creative patchwork

Hanne Wellendorph

ARCO PUBLISHING, INC.
NEW YORK

Published by Arco Publishing, Inc.
215 Park Avenue South, New York, N.Y. 10003

Copyright © 1985 by Hanne Wellendorph

Library of Congress Cataloging in Publication Data

Wellendorph, Hanne.
    Creative patchwork.

    1. Patchwork.   I. Title.
TT835.W46 1985   746.46   85-1443
ISBN 0-668-06200-2 (Paper Edition)

Printed in the United States of America

10   9   8   7   6   5   4   3   2   1

CONTENTS

FOREWORD

Patchwork Philosophy

This book is meant to be an inspiration to everybody, and so it emphasizes creativity rather than technical accomplishments. Sewing machine techniques have been included along with hand-sewing techniques in order to meet today's demand for quick and durable work. Used appropriately and with accuracy, the sewing machine can provide a product as genuine and as beautiful as hand-made needlework.

Patchwork is an old craft with many traditions. According to the dictionary, a *patch* is "a part, a shred, or a piece," and *work* means "a task." As a compound word, *patchwork* tells us that this form of needlework consists of some patches sewn or worked together seam by seam. Therefore, a distinction can be made between patchwork and other needlework that involves fabric, like appliqué.

Many museums in Britain and America have lovely old quilts on display that bear witness to the great patience and economy of their makers. Nothing was discarded: even the smallest pieces of material, irrespective of quality, might be sewn in patchwork and contribute to a useful and beautiful whole.

Many techniques used for patchwork today have roots in the past, but our choice of material has changed. We often buy fabric for our "compositions" in order to get the colors and effects we want even at the expense of utility. But in my opinion, the time spent grappling with material, pattern, and color is very important! When one becomes engrossed and fascinated by the working process, one forgets all about time and place. The soul is moved, and the creative spirit emerges. We are all creative, only to various degrees. We have what amounts to an obligation, in fact, to use this inborn creativity to enhance our lives and the lives of those around us.

INTRODUCTION

Working Methods

I have found that I can best sew crisp, accurate patchwork by using the simplified method of patchwork piecing described on the following pages. I baste fabric around pattern paper and then sew the finished pieces of my patchwork design together. The method resembles "English piecing," except that the pattern papers are not caught in the final overcast stitching that joins the pieces of fabric together, and the papers are removed once the basting stitches are taken out. Although this method involves the seemingly "extra" step of basting, I think you will find, as I have, that the time saved by not having to rip and resew inaccurate piecing and the consistently fine results you can achieve with this method make the basting more than worthwhile.

The Techniques explain my general method of doing patchwork one step at a time. Next come simple projects that give you practice with these working methods, and then instructions are given for many exciting patchwork projects, from wall-hangings to purses to Christmas decorations. Finally, I have given general instructions for finishing or mounting patchwork projects that supplement or provide alternatives to the finishing techniques described with each set of instructions. You may find it useful to read the information about materials at the end of the book *before* you begin, and you can consult the Glossary as you work through the projects if you see terms that are unfamiliar to you. Measurements are given in inches with metric equivalents throughout. Measurements given with the instructions are suitable for four-squares-to-the-inch pattern paper.

TECHNIQUES

Technique 1: Cutting, Basting, and Hand-Stitching Patchwork

This technique is used for all hand-sewn patchwork for which pattern paper is used, whatever the shape of the patches. It is easiest to work with pattern paper marked out in squares: right angles are already there for you to use, and once you count how many squares to an inch or centimeter you have on your paper, you can cut without drawing or measuring. See page 86 for more about pattern paper.

a. Cut the number of shapes required by your pattern or design from the pattern paper (other techniques to follow explain how to draw your pattern and how to mark the pieces to use them in patchwork, and so forth).

b. Choose fabric and cut it to the measurements of your pattern paper shapes plus ⅜ inch (1 cm) for seam allowance. Pin the fabric carefully around the paper pattern pieces.

c. Baste the material around each paper, sewing through both material and paper. Be sure that the material fits snugly around the paper edges, and that the corners are neat when the piece is turned right-side-up. Get used to leaving the knot on the face of the piece: you will be removing the basting stitches later. Edges marked with a wavy line to indicate the outside edge of your design (see page 8) need not be basted: they will be finished when you mount your work on a backing or liner.

d. Press all the small pieces—if possible, use a steam iron.

e. Place the small patchwork units in front of you and lay them out in the design you want. Play with the arrangement until the shape and colors suit you.

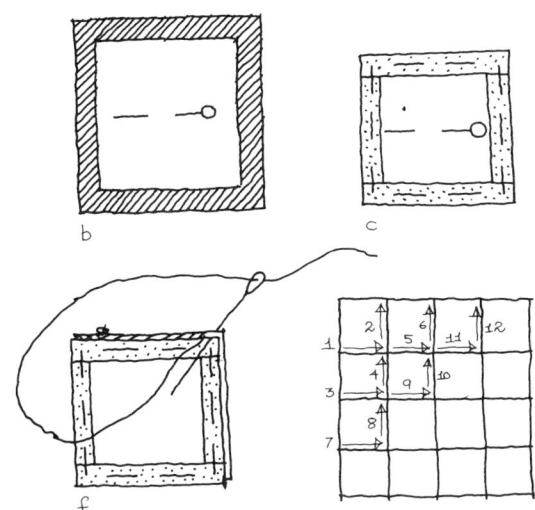

Follow the arrows when stitching together.

f. Sew the units together with sewing thread that matches your fabric. Use a fine needle (number 8 embroidery needles work well). Place the pieces side by side, as snugly as you can without distorting them, and sew with small, tight, overcast stitches. Begin about ¼ inch (6 mm) in from the edge; sew about three stitches moving toward the edge (in the "wrong" direction), and then sew forward along the joined edges. When you begin each new thread, and at all corners, sew a couple of stitches in the same place (that is, on top of each other), but do not break the thread. If the stitches are too obvious on the right side, use a finer needle and somewhat tighter stitches, or use smaller stitches. *Squares are sewn together on the wrong side in zigzag* (see figure f). Catch *only* the fabric when you stitch, not the paper inside.

g. Press the whole work and remove the pattern papers. If necessary, press again (from the front).

1

Technique 2: Constructing Shapes

For figures with angles that are not right angles (90°—see Glossary), you will have to make your own patterns. Use heavy gray cardboard (the kind used for tablet backs will do: do *not* use corrugated cardboard). Draw with ruler, compass, and a pencil directly onto the cardboard and cut out the pattern piece with a hobby knife. After cutting, all the drawings onto pattern paper will be made using the cardboard pieces—so you will have to be very careful and exact with your cardboard patterns or your pieces will not fit together properly later.

To Raise a Perpendicular from a Given Point:

A perpendicular line is a straight line that meets another straight line at a right angle. Draw a small circle, centered at C, so that it intersects a horizontal line at points A and B. Setting the compass arm so that the radius is about the desired point over C, draw a circle (or part of it) with A as the center, and another circle with B as the center. Finally, connect the point where these two circles intersect with C, using a ruler.

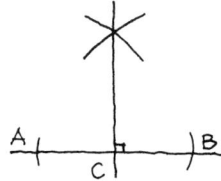

to raise
a perpendicular

To Bisect an Angle:

Draw a circle with C as center. Mark points A and B along the circle so that straight lines drawn to them from C make an angle of the desired size. Then use your compass to make two circles with a longer radius than the circle drawn from C, one centered at A and one at B. Draw a line through the intersection of the circles; this line will divide the angle into two equal angles.

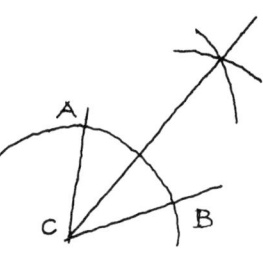

to bisect
an angle

To Bisect a Line Segment:

Start with a horizontal line, and mark on it two points at some distance from one another, A and B. Draw a suitably wide circle with A as center, and a similar circle with B as center. Connect the points where the two circles intersect above and below the line. Line AB is cut in half and the line segment is therefore bisected.

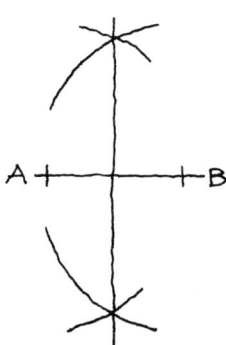

to bisect
a line segment

Triangle

Points and circles will intersect at D, C, and E. Connect D and C, D and B, and C and B, with a ruler, and you will have a triangle with equal sides. Use a hobby knife to cut out this triangle.

Diamond or "Harlequin"

Mark the center "C" with a cross and draw a circle with a radius equal to about 2 inches (5 cm). Mark B at some point along the circumference of this circle and draw another circle the same size with center B. Points and circles will again intersect at points D, C, and E. Connect D and C, C and E, E and B, and B and D—and get a diamond or rhombus, also sometimes called a "harlequin." Cut out.

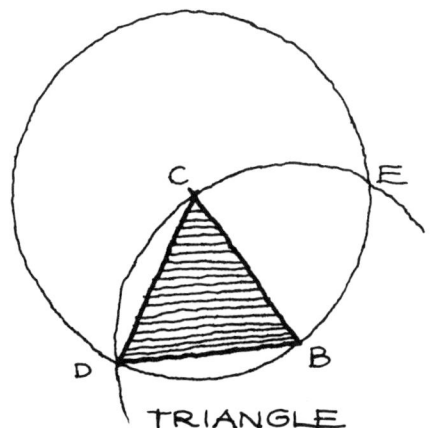

TRIANGLE

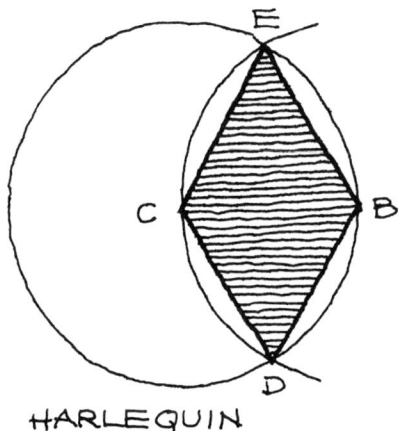

HARLEQUIN

Pentagon

Mark two points on a horizontal line, A and B, about 2 inches (5 cm) apart, to make line AB. Bisect AB as explained on page 10, and mark 2 inches (5 cm) on this line, at right angles to AB. This is point C. Draw a line from B upward past C, and mark ½ AB (here 1 inch [2.5 cm]) upward from C on this line, point D. With centers in B and A, draw two circular arcs with radius equal to DB. The intersecting point of the circles—E—will then appear on the middle line that bisects AB. From E, the sides of the pentagon can be marked on circular arcs, using a radius equal to AB (here 2 inches [5 cm]). Finally, draw the last two sides. Cut out.

Hexagon

Draw a circle with a radius of 2 inches (5 cm). Mark a point F somewhere along the circumference and mark the distance (equal to the radius) between the legs of the compass six times on the circumference of the circle as shown in the diagram, moving counterclockwise. Connect the points, and you have a hexagon with sides of 2 inches (5 cm) each. Cut out.

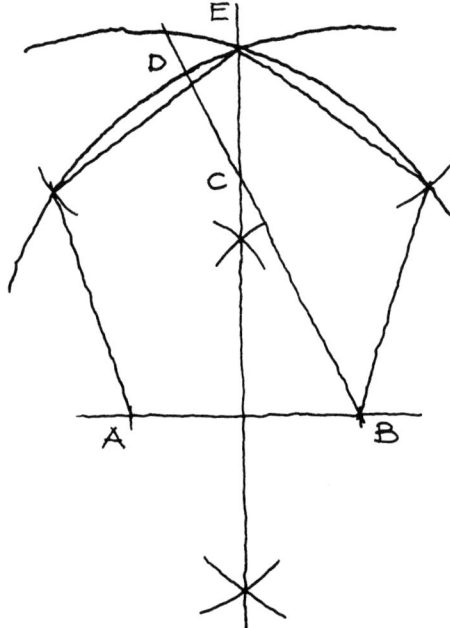

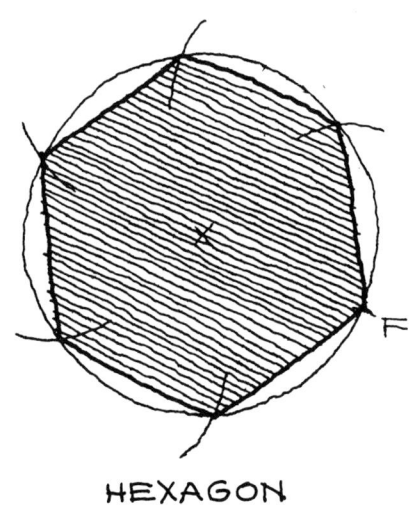

HEXAGON

Octagon

Draw a circle with a radius of 2 inches (5 cm). Draw the horizontal diameter and then draw a perpendicular line from the center C (see page 4). Extend line DC downward until it intersects the circle, point E. Then bisect the right angle between E and B (thus also bisecting the angle between D and A). In the same way, bisect the angle between E and A (and therefore D and B). Connect the marked points on the circle. Cut out.

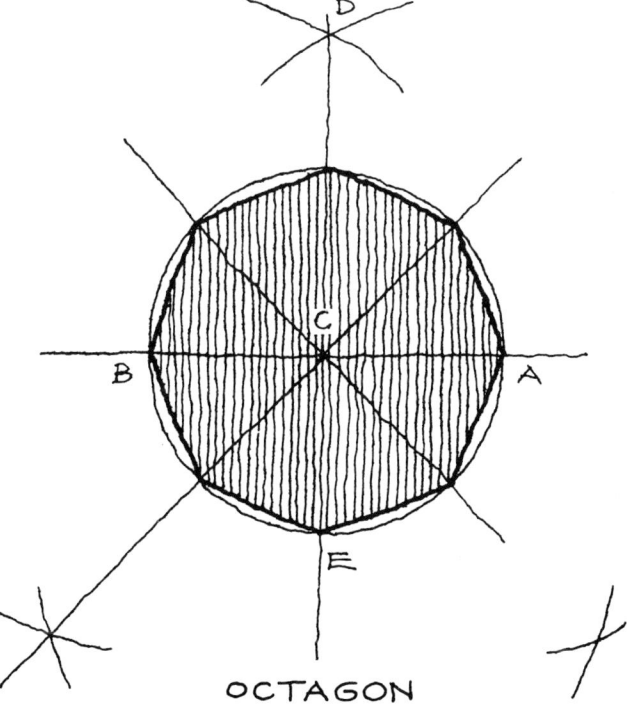

OCTAGON

Dodecagon (Twelve-Sided Figure)

Draw a hexagon and bisect the angles.

Sixteen-Sided Figure

Draw an octagon and bisect the angles.

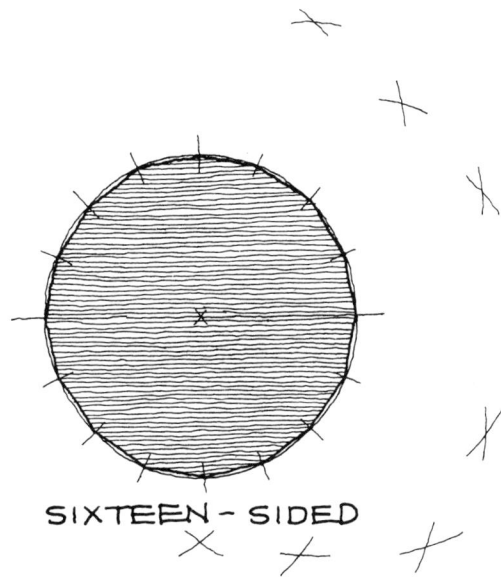

SIXTEEN - SIDED

Once you have mastered these figures, there are countless ways in which to combine them. If the finished result is to be appliquéd on material, replace the paper backing with interfacing. Cut the interfacing the exact size of the pattern piece (no seam allowance should be added), but don't forget that the result may be somewhat stiff.

Suggestions:
Sew six triangles into a flower.
Sew twelve pentagons into a patchwork ball.
Sew six harlequins (diamonds) into a star.
Sew seven hexagons into a flower with a center.

Technique 3: Combining Shapes

You can make your own designs by combining various shapes with the same side measures.

Some shapes combined give spacious designs; pentagons and hexagons, for example, combine very well. Test your combinations in paper before you cut fabric.

Combi-Star

a. Draw and cut according to patterns, all with sides equal to one-quarter of the diameter desired for the finished star:
   six triangles
   one hexagon
   six diamonds (harlequins)
b. Choose three pieces of material, preferably contrasting colors, for the triangles.
c. Sew together, using patchwork Technique 1. See page 84 for instructions for basting acute angles.
d. Sew a lot of combi-stars together to form a complete sky!

Technique 4: Composing Your Own Patterns

If you have some kind of inspiration for a simple and good drawing or design with straight lines that might be suitable for patchwork, but cannot be directly fitted into a pattern, try applying this technique. Say, for instance, you have drawn a human face. Look closely at your draft and work with it as follows:

a. Transfer your drawing into a piece of cardboard or stiff paper. Draw it large enough to make it possible for you to sew the individual pieces together, and make it adaptable to various colors and fabrics.
b. With a ruler and sharply pointed pencil, turn all curved lines into straight lines—but be sure not to create too many sharp edges.
c. Divide the large areas into smaller ones, again being sure to avoid angles that are too acute.
d. Compare your sketch with the patchwork pattern you have worked out. If necessary, make corrections to obtain the desired effect.
e. Continue, following Technique 5.

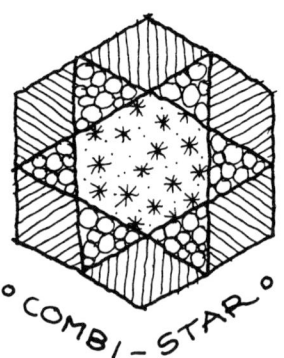

This is a rapid
scribble or doodle
—and the resulting
mask.

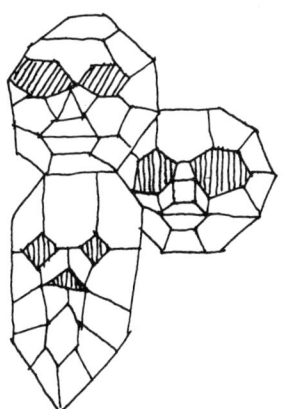

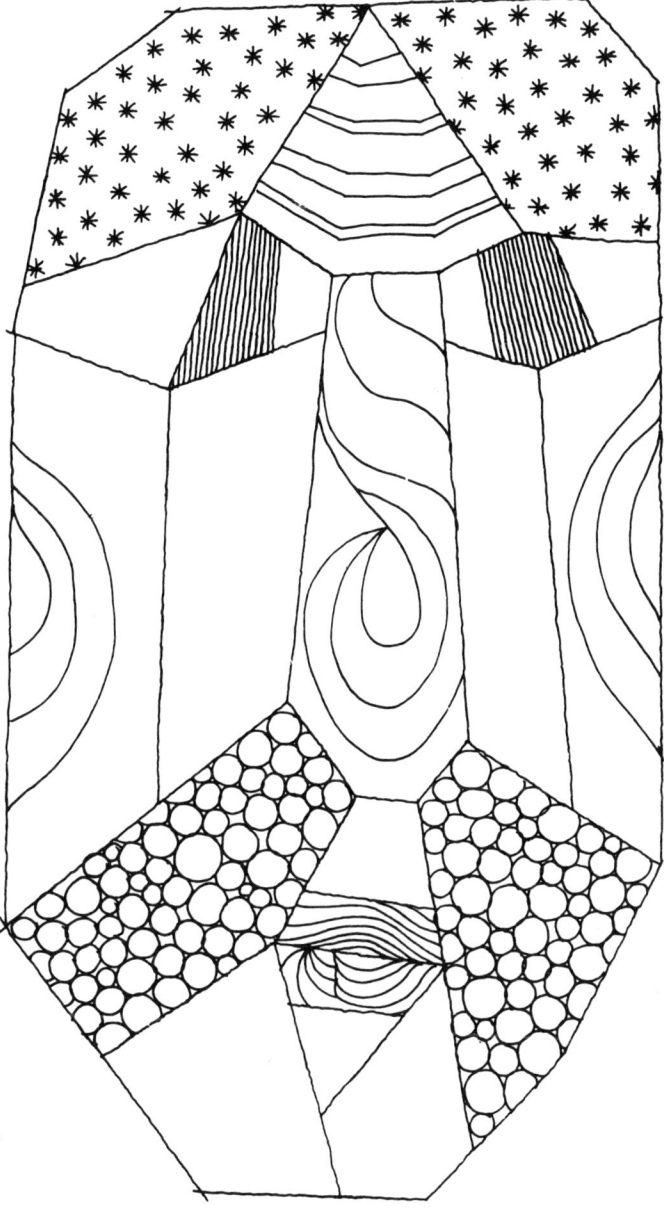

The mask has been
sewn together and
used as decoration for
a Spanish carry-all.

Technique 5: Marking Your Own Design

Once you have a pattern of your own in the size you want, such as a thoroughly worked-out draft (Technique 4) or a pattern drawn directly on suitable paper with pencil and ruler, proceed as follows:

a. Choose fabric. Use wool, silk, and linen if you like, as long as the finished work is not to be washed.

b. Mark with capital letters all parts for which the same material is to be used (if necessary, indicate the nap). See the figure: A, B, C indicate different fabrics. Mark the location of each piece with numerals: 1, 2, 3, 4, for example, so that A1, A2, and A3 indicate for you that the same fabric is being used in particular places in your design. Mark the edges of pattern pieces that fall along the outer edge of the design with a wavy line.

c. Make a quick little working drawing with the same number and letter markings as the original.

d. Cut out and sew together, following patchwork Technique 1.

You will find it very helpful to use bulletin board material or decorator cork blocks covered with linen or canvas to lay out your patchwork pieces with pins before sewing them together.

The "Diagonal" pillow (see instructions for a variation on page 58) can be drawn directly on pattern paper and finished following Technique 5.

Note that your pattern will become laterally reversed (see page 73) if you mark the top side and baste the material on the opposite side. However, this is unimportant if the pattern is symmetrical.

In asymmetrical patterns (patterns that don't fall into two halves corresponding exactly around a center),

the individual parts are lifted and marked on the reverse side after each has been cut out. The fabric is basted on the top side; that is, as it was first mounted.

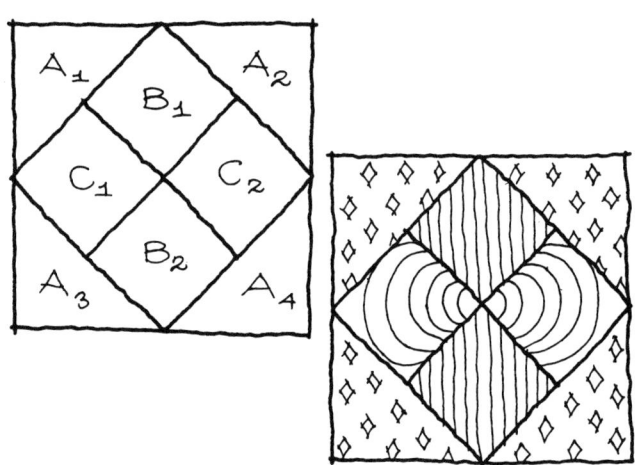

8

Technique 6: Enlarging

A pattern drawn on graph paper or any kind of grid can be enlarged for patchwork. To do this, use checked pattern paper or draw your own grid on heavy wrapping paper, around which the fabric can be basted directly.

Compare the size of the squares in your pattern with those of the pattern paper: look at the length of the sides, decide the approximate size of the finished work, and experiment until you have the size you want.

This module (a module is simply a unit of a design) is intended for a small tapestry.

Example 1: If □ = 2 squares on paper, you'll have to count
3 × 2 squares across and
3 × 2 squares upward for a pattern twice the size of the original.

Example 2: If □ = 3 squares on paper, you'll have to count
3 × 3 squares across and
3 × 3 squares upward for a pattern three times the size of the original.

Example 3: If □ = 4 squares on paper, you'll have to count
3 × 4 squares across and
3 × 4 squares upward for a pattern four times the size of the original.

Draw in the design of the module, multiplying the number of squares used for each line in the module by the number giving the enlargement you've chosen: two for twice as large, and so forth. Which enlargement is the right one depends on the purpose of your draft. If it is intended as a pattern for a tapestry, you have to calculate the size of the module compared with the size desired for the finished work. Also, take a look at the individual parts: pieces that are too small are very difficult to sew; pieces that are too large may be further divided, thus changing the look of the pattern. For more about dividing pattern units, see page 91. All my tapestries started as patterns on checkered paper—often drawn in moments when I found teaching or conversation boring. Many people "compose" their best work while on the telephone!

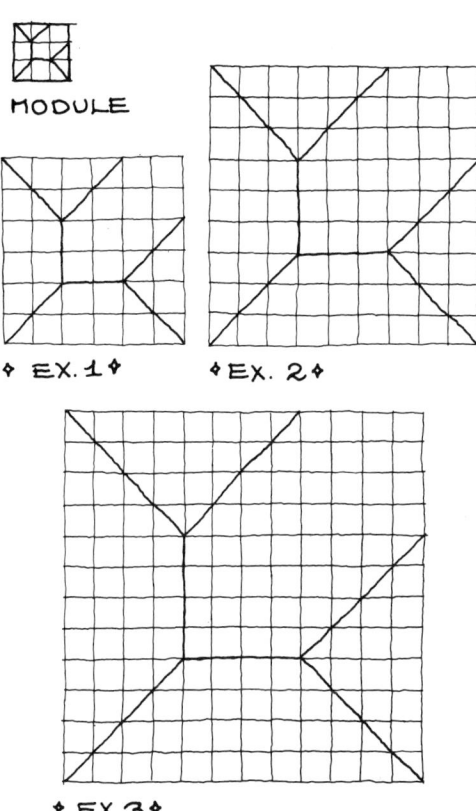

MODULE

✦ EX. 1 ✦   ✦ EX. 2 ✦

✦ EX. 3 ✦

Technique 7: Machine-Sewing Strips Together

Tear strips; then cut a piece of medium-weight fabric (sheeting, for example) to be used as a ground material or backing to the desired size. Iron all the pieces, then mount the strips on the backing, sewing patchwork as follows:

a. Place the first strip on the edge of the backing, right-side-up. Baste or pin. Let the strip overlap the edges as you sew, then trim to about ¼ inch (6 mm) from the backing edge.

b. The second strip is placed over the first strip, right sides together (and with the wrong side facing up). Fasten with pins and stitch ¼ inch (6 mm) from the long edge (threads that have frayed never included). Use the sewing machine presser foot as a guide.

c. Remove pins, open right-side-out, and press the strip in place (preferably with a steam iron). Cut off the strip a little from the edge as before.

d. The third strip is placed on the second one, right sides together and wrong-side-up; fasten with pins and stitch ¼ inch (6 mm) from the edge.

e. Remove pins, unfold, press. Continue like this until your entire ground material is covered with strips.

f. Sew a line of ordinary stitching just inside the backing edge all the way around. Trim frayed edges and press if necessary.

Machine sewing is very exacting, and you must do the following:

- Tear all material. Therefore, use suitable fabric, such as cottons.
- Estimate all material from the first lengthwise thread inside the frayed threads. Not all materials are woven with the same tightness, and fabrics may fray differently.
- Always iron in the direction of the threads—that is, vertically or horizontally, not diagonally—in order to avoid pulling the fabric out of shape.

This technique is very applicable to the decoration of clothing such as sleeves and pockets. If desired, place a "peekaboo" border of bias strips between the patchwork strips, sewing directly to the backing.

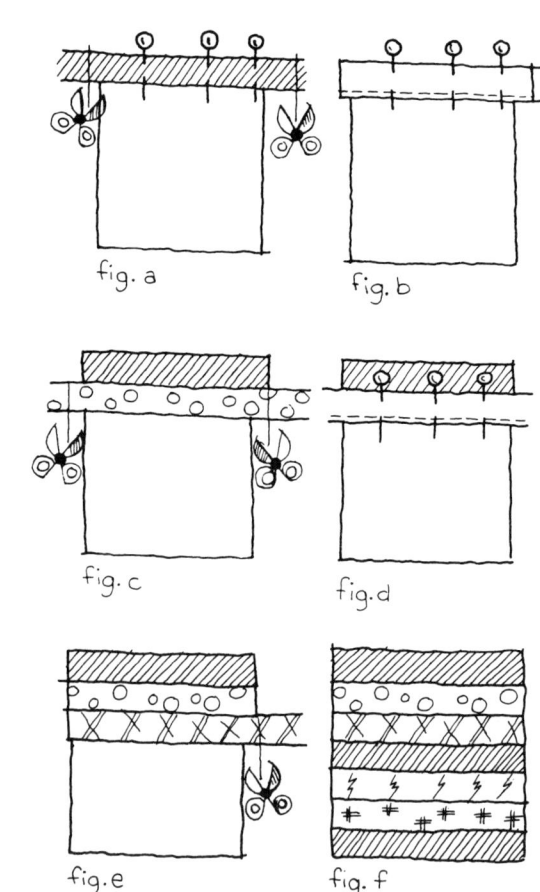

fig. a   fig. b

fig. c   fig. d

fig. e   fig. f

Technique 8: Machine-Sewing Squares Together

a. Tear strips according to the measurements required by your pattern and iron them.

b. Divide the strip into squares or rectangles by cutting the material to measure, following the threads to cut along the grain of the fabric.

c. Place the squares in a pattern and move them around until the pattern looks nice. Position cut-edge along cut-edge and tear-edge along tear-edge.

d. Mark the first square in each row by pinning on a slip of paper (see figure *d*) and stack the squares for each row together.

e. Sew the squares together in strips, cut-edge to cut-edge, face-to-face, with a ¼-inch (6-mm) seam allowance. On the wrong side, press the seams open, and then iron the whole strip from the front. Keep the paper markers.

f. Sew the rest of the piles together in strips and iron as described above.

g. Finish the sewing as described for Technique 7. Pin all seams to keep the correct shape.

If you want to sew large tapestries, shirts, and so forth, that are to be lined, this technique is especially suitable, as the lining can be the ground material. Machine-made patchwork often wears very well.

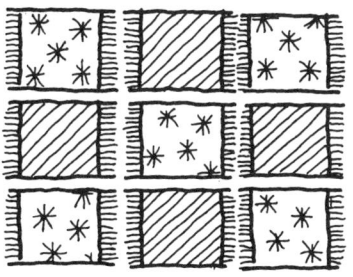

fig. c

fig. d

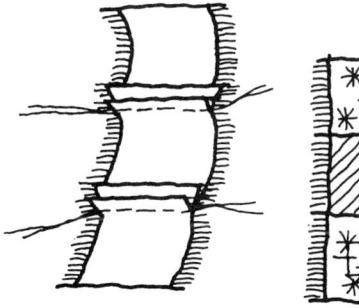

fig. e

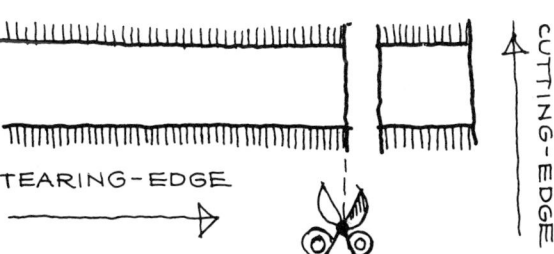

TEARING-EDGE

CUTTING-EDGE

11

Technique 9: Sewing a "Log Cabin"

This sophisticated form of patchwork has very old roots. If you choose material mainly in two sharply contrasting colors, dark and light colors, for example, there are exciting ways of combining the blocks into larger, striking color patterns.

a. Tear the material into strips and cut the ground material as described for Technique 7. Cut a center square to the dimensions desired plus ½ inch (12 mm) across and down. Iron.

b. Fold in diagonal lines on your ground cloth to guide your stitching, folding your ground-cloth square in half diagonally first from one corner and then from the opposite corner. You should see a clear X. Mount the starting square so that the corners fall on the diagonal lines on all four corners.

c. Sew the strips onto the ground cloth (Technique 7) along the edges of the center piece in turn, working from the center out according to the diagram. Use the vertical and horizontal threads and the center square as a guide to keep your sewing straight.

d. Since the Log Cabin is built up around the center square, you can vary the design by positioning the square in various ways and sewing on the strips as desired. See some variations on pages 13 and 14.

e. The center shape can also be a triangle, an octagon, or a hexagon. You'll find, however, that blocks of Log Cabin work best together when all the blocks in a given piece have the same center shape.

fig. b, c

12

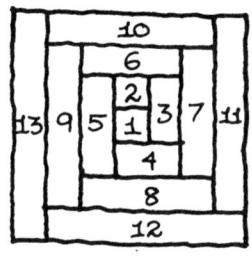

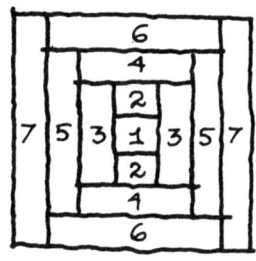

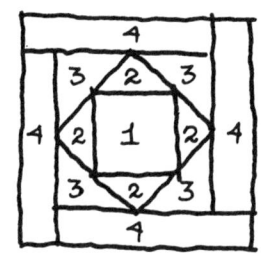

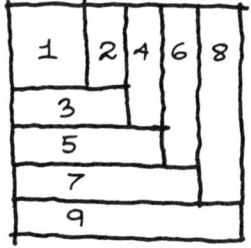

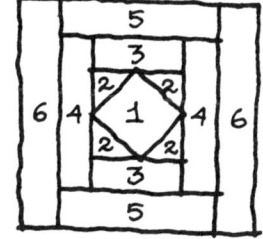

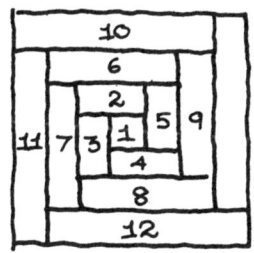

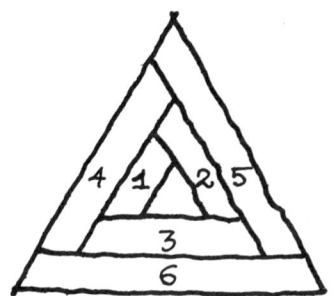

13

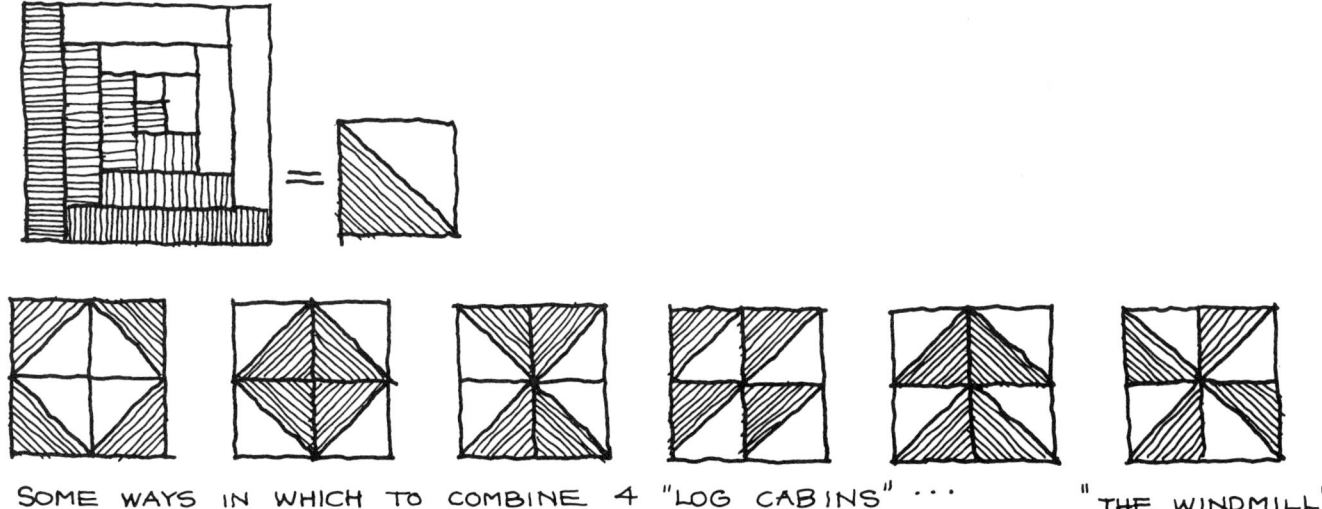

SOME WAYS IN WHICH TO COMBINE 4 "LOG CABINS" ··· "THE WINDMILL"

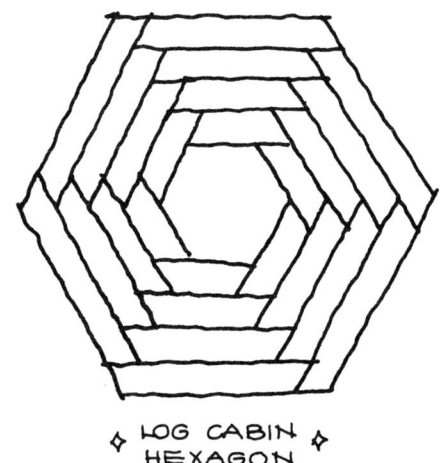

◇ LOG CABIN ◇
HEXAGON

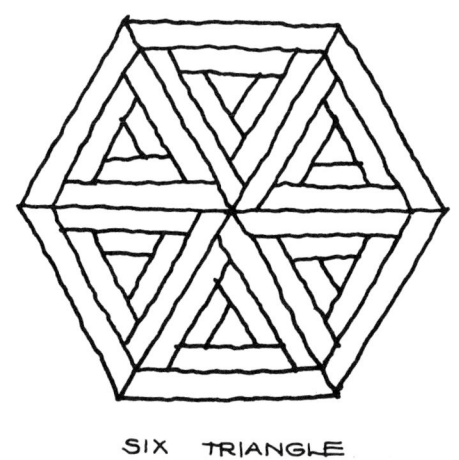

SIX TRIANGLE
"LOG CABINS"

Technique 10: Making Patchwork
Bias Strips

If you want a finishing touch for your work, sew decorative bias strips from scraps of fabric. The left-overs from the patchwork you are finishing make an excellent border.

With a little practice, you will have a uniform, bias-cut ribbon.

a. Narrow and broad widths of cotton strips cut along the grain of the fabric are lined up together for the most economical use of fabric. Stagger each width of fabric a bit downward from the strip next to it as shown.

b. Stitch the pieces together with the sewing machine, right sides together, and press the seams to the same side, being careful to sew straight along grain lines.

c. With a ruler and pencil, mark the desired width along the bias of the sewn strips. Then cut your bias ribbon.

d. Stitch the ribbons together into one long ribbon.

e. Fold the edges under and press, being sure that the seam allowances from joining your strips lie flat. A hem guide will make this task very much easier.

f. Use the ribbon like an ordinary bias strip (see page 82).

A bias strip has been used to finish the Christmas runner and the placemat shown on page 37.

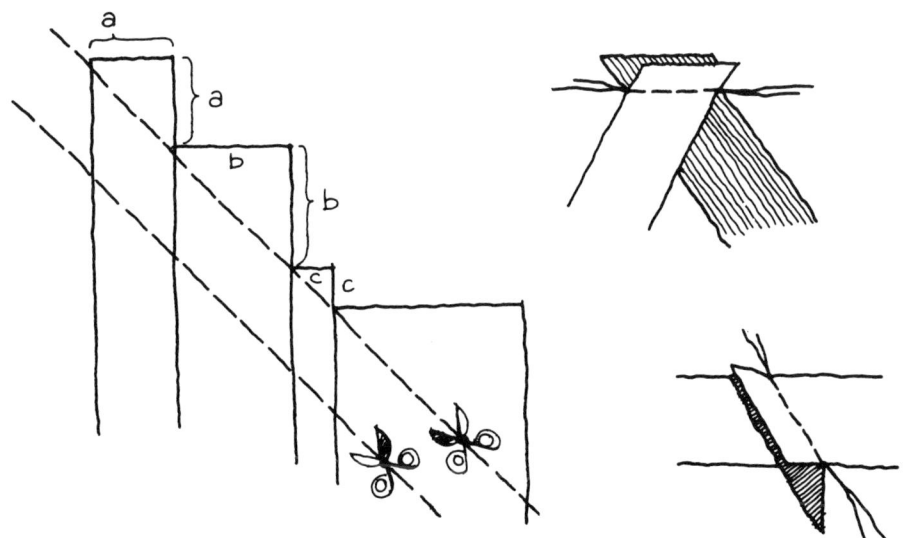

AFTER STITCHING,
THE CORNERS ARE TRIMMED.

15

INCENTIVES
Flowers

Go for a walk, breathe in the fresh air, and gather the flowers of the season.

On a piece of graph paper or a grid, you now draw a flower. What are the characteristics of the flower? Its form? Its petals? Its layout—its colors—its leaves? Are you able to divide it into four, five, six, or many uniform parts? Look, for instance, at the number of petals.

Make an attempt to draw the flower. Start in the middle. If necessary, draw some extra circles to help you keep a uniform shape. As shown below, I drew concentric circles divided into ten segments, and then shaped edges, making five segments.

You can draw a daffodil, for example, by drawing two such circles, one small and one large. Adapting the size to your flower, draw six marks on the big circle to make a hexagon (Technique 2) and make use of this to draw the outer, yellow petals. When you have a usable draft or sketch, just follow the technique for enlargement, and so forth. Then try to choose colors close to those of nature.

Spread the flowers on a table runner or a cushion.

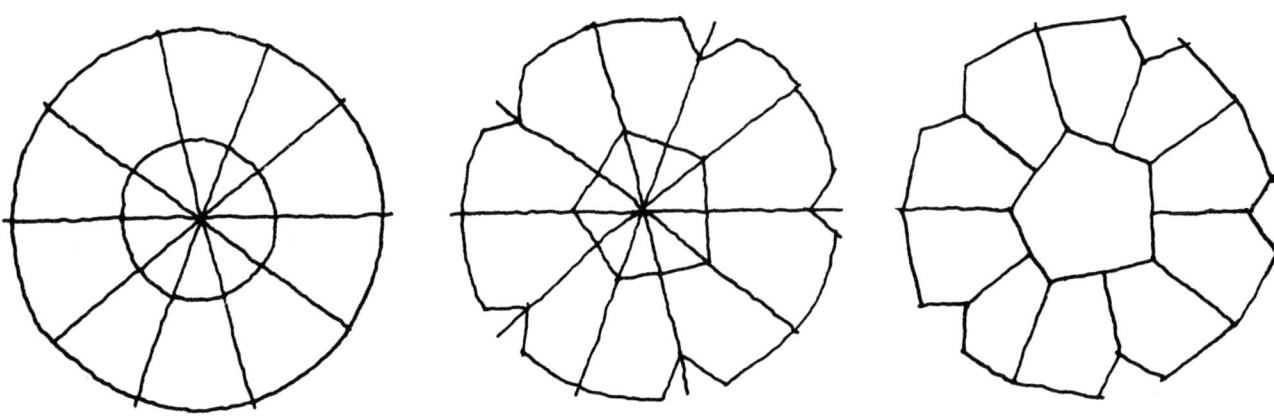

For hearts, see page 30.

18

Bedspread

A bedspread is a major project because it is so large, and if the result is to justify your time and costs, you'll have to spend quite awhile on the preliminary work—the pattern and choice of colors. When you have created your pattern and carefully selected materials, the actual sewing together will pose no serious difficulties.

The pattern consists of some primary modules or shapes, drawn first, and secondary shapes popping up between the primary ones.

For a large bedspread, draw large primary shapes; those for a child's bedspread should be smaller.

Referring to page 21:

a. Draw a circle with a radius of about 2 inches (5 cm).
b. Work first on the outside edges. The lines must not be too short; try for a minimum of two squares. If necessary, notch the edge—your design need not look like a circle.
c. Center a square in the middle of the figure.
d. Divide the spaces between the center and the outer edge into geometric shapes. Form a pattern.
e. Draw another three modules or basic shapes like your first one (Step b) and join them together. They must touch along some edges.
f. Fill in the rest of the pattern on the other three modules.
g. Make a pattern in the space between the four modules.
h. Convert to actual size (Technique 6).

Decide on a color scheme and sew a sample module of your primary and your secondary shape before you commit yourself to your first choice of color and fabric.

For a large or small bedspread, you should wash all fabrics and iron them before you start sewing.

Also, consider quilting your bedspread (see page 81).

The color photograph on page 20 shows a variation of this design, which is graphed on page 23.

□ = 5 squares in my bedspread; that is, the primary module measures about 12½ inches (31.75 cm) in diameter; and my bedspread consists of 30 primary modules and 20 secondary modules, plus 18 half-secondary modules, and rounded borders. The result is a 62½ × 75-inch (158-cm × 190.5-cm) spread—5 × 6 primary modules. This is fine for a double bed. A twin-size bed requires only 4 × 6 primary modules.

Look at some other ways of dividing primary and secondary modules on pages 22 and 23.

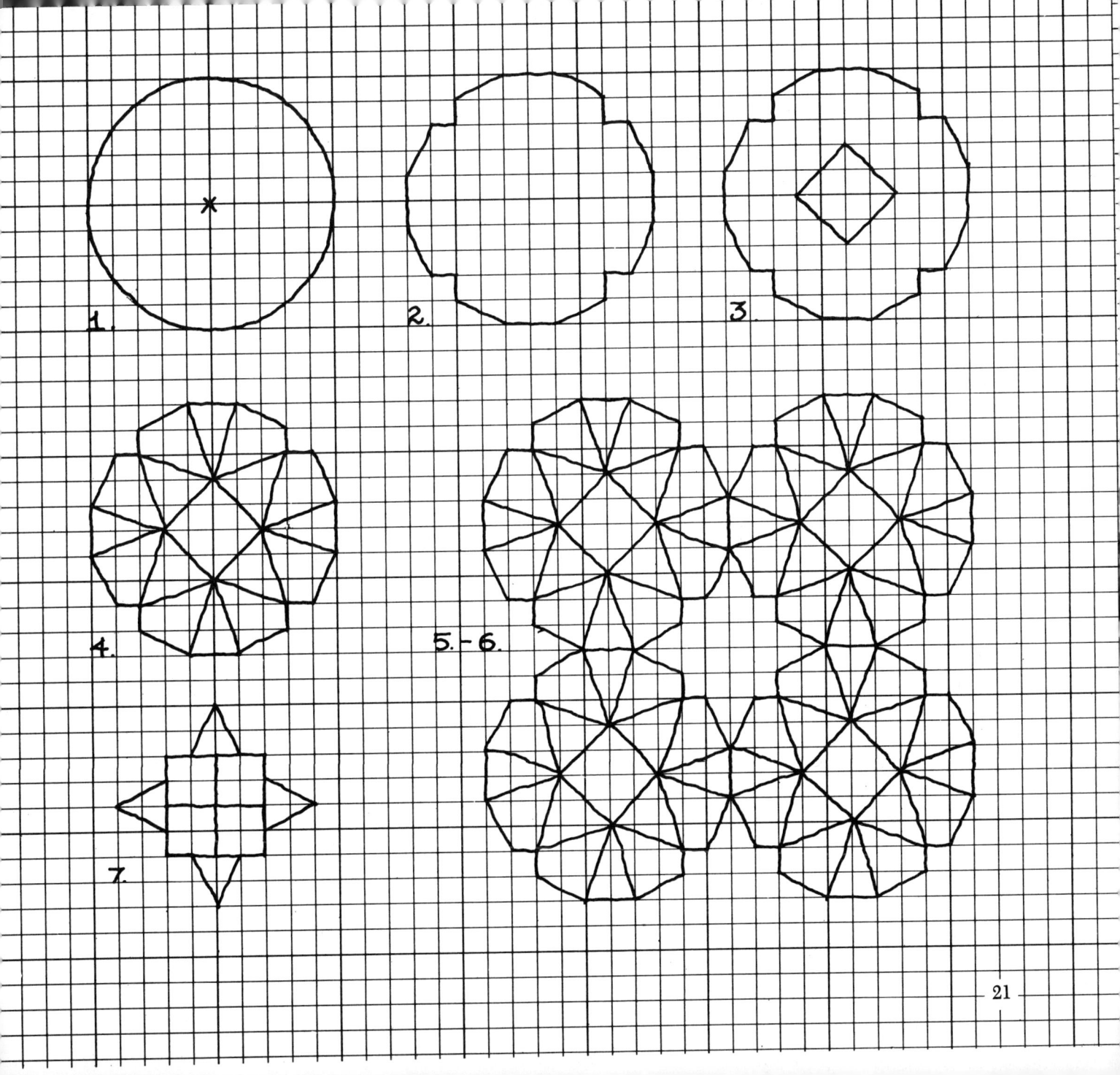

1.

2.

3.

4.

5. - 6.

7.

21

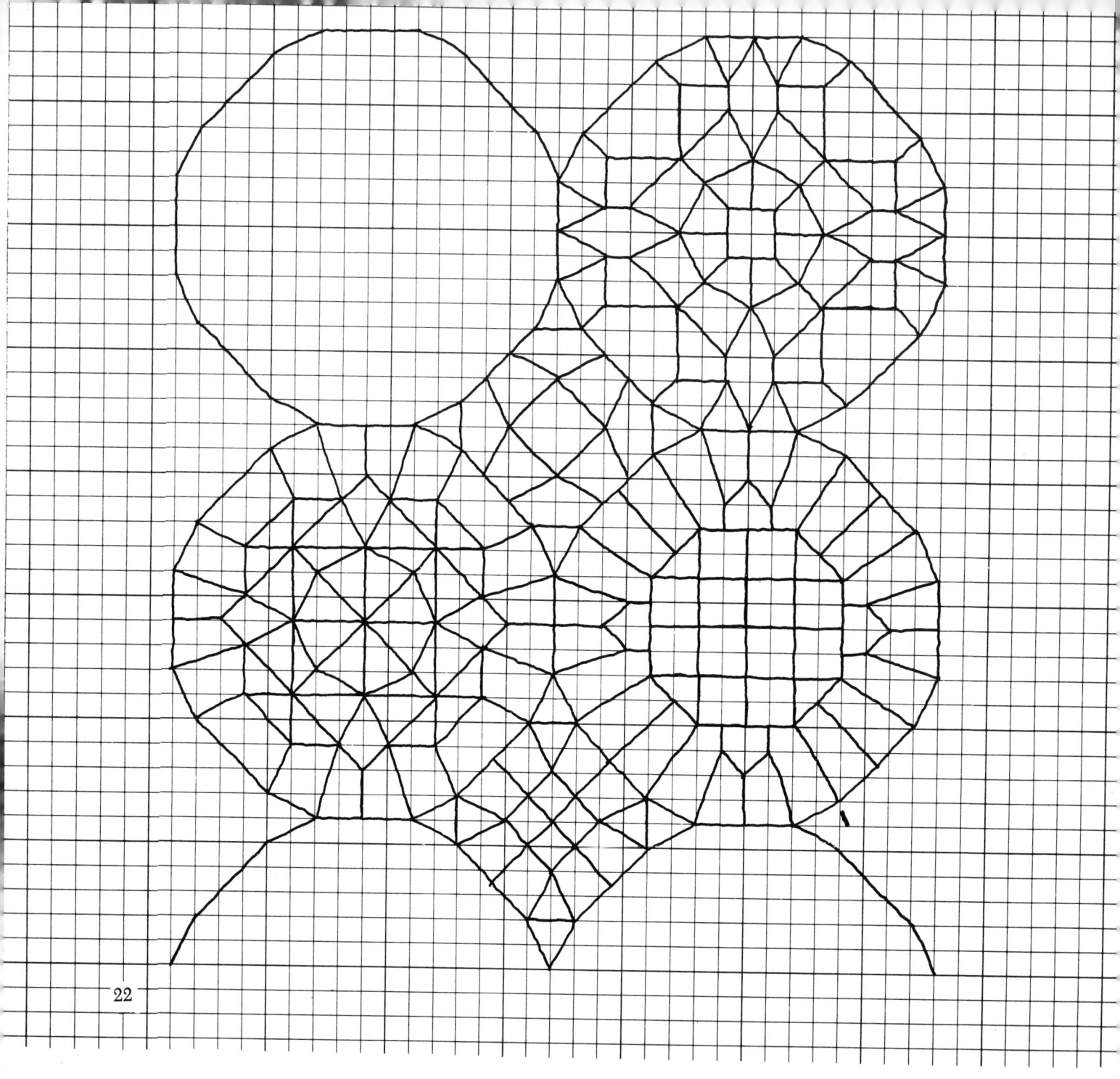

22

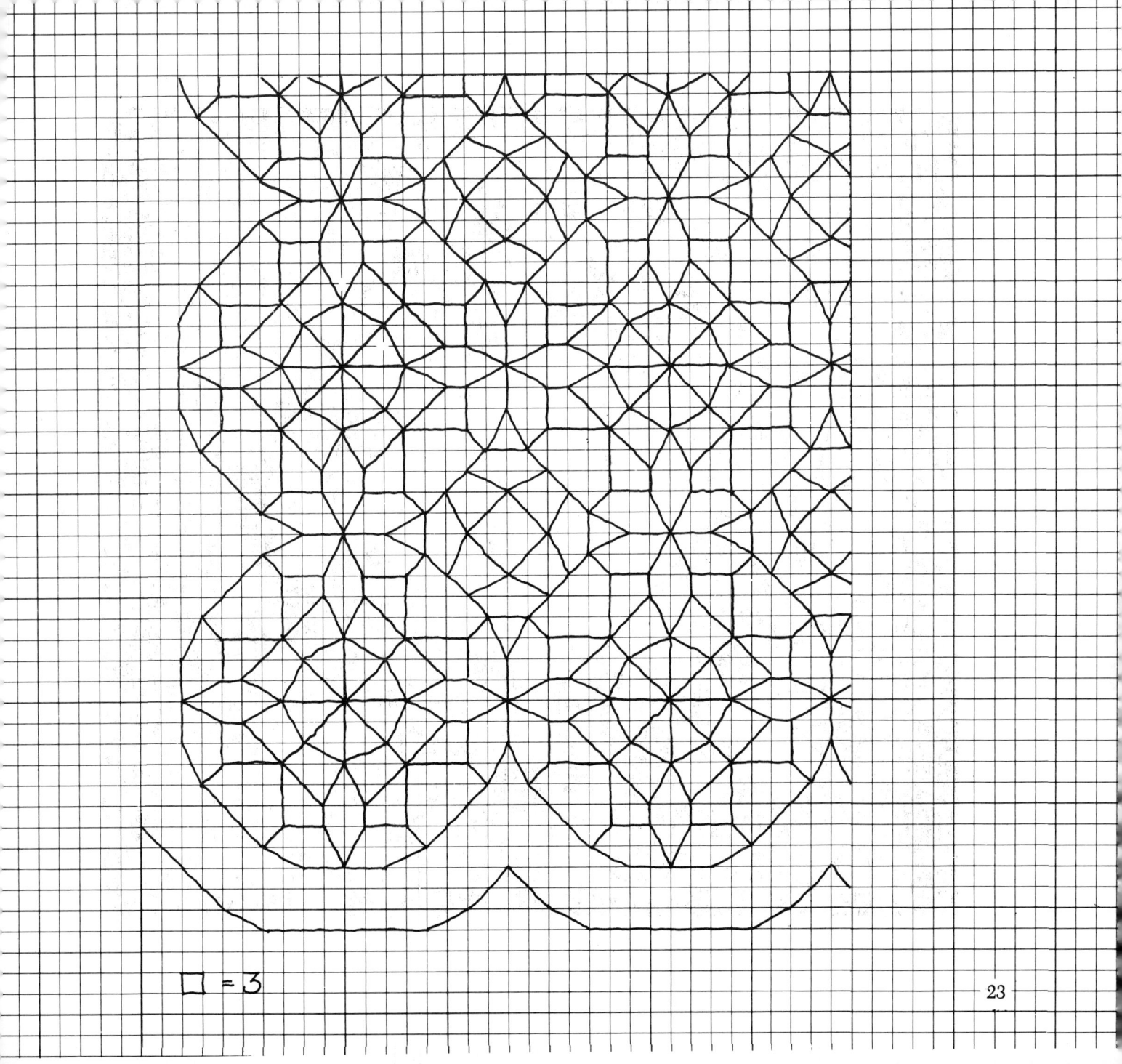

□ = 3

23

See pages 26 and 27.

My bellpull is a
sampler of patchwork
blocks, all the same
size and made from the
same fabrics.

Small Coverlet (Cradle or Bassinet Size)

A small coverlet needs small modules, perhaps primary and fill-in shapes of the same size. The bassinet coverlet shown is set in a border and machine-quilted (see page 81).

Draw your own pattern on graph paper as follows:

a. Draw a square over 7 × 7 grid squares and center a square of 3 × 3 squares inside it.

b. Connect the central section with the outer lines in a simple way. By "cutting" the corners at an angle, it is possible to form secondary shapes; the more you "cut," the bigger the secondary modules. If necessary, divide your primary shape still further.

c. Draw another three primary modules adjoining one another. Divide the secondary modules into separate parts. If you have mainly horizontal/vertical lines in the primary modules, diagonal lines will be nicest in the secondary modules (or vice versa).

d. Adjust the shapes until you are satisfied with the design.

Color your pattern; enlarge it (Technique 6)—with an enlargement of □ = 3, 4 × 7 primary modules give 21 inches × 36¾ inches (53.25 cm × 93.25 cm), which is about bassinet size; you can add rows of modules to length or width to make the coverlet larger. Stitch an experimental block (Techniques 5 and 1)—and *do* wash the materials you've chosen before proceeding to piece your coverlet.

Frequently, you can simply fill in along the outside border, or try to devise a border of your own (on graph paper first) for a special finishing touch.

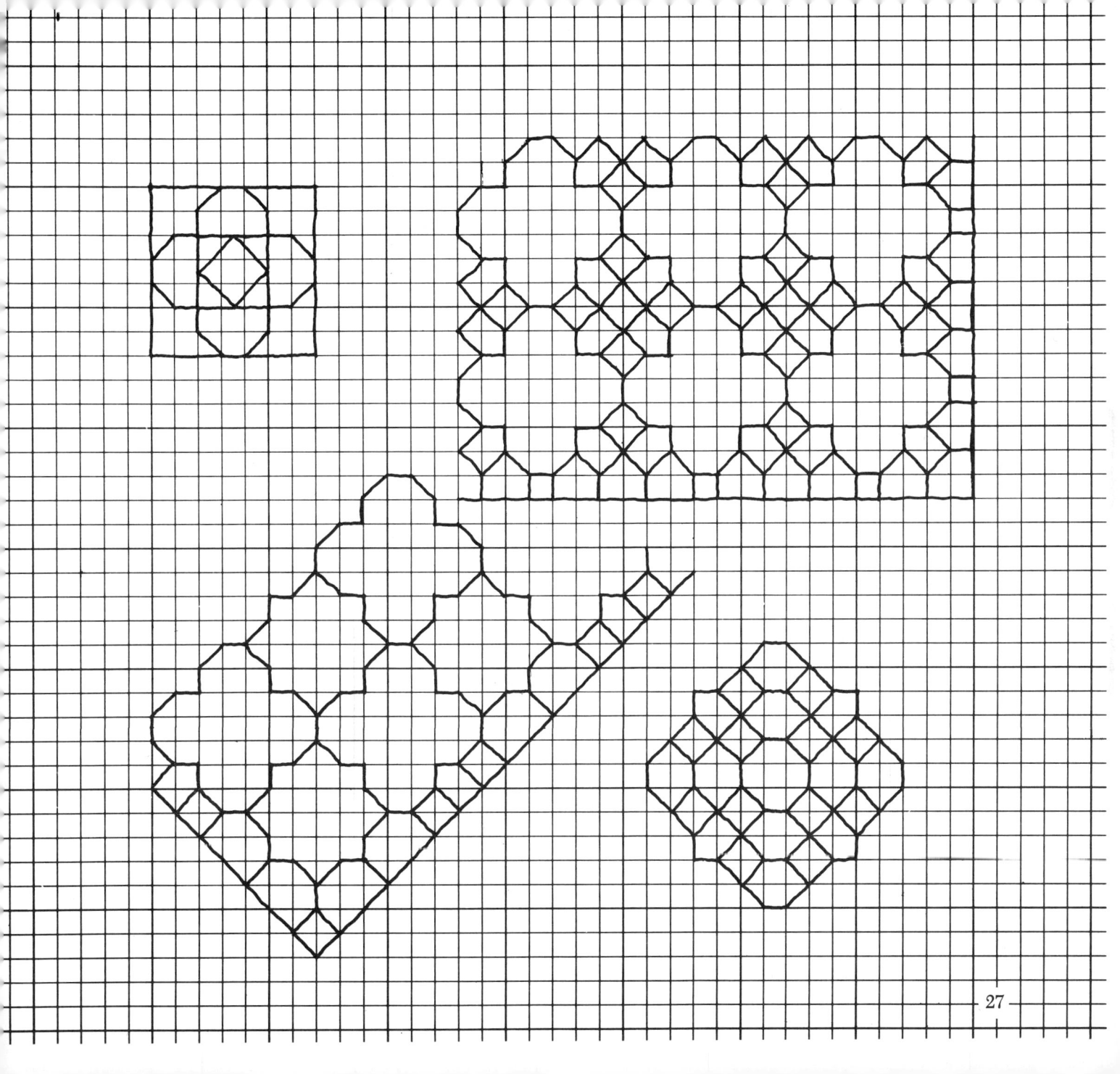

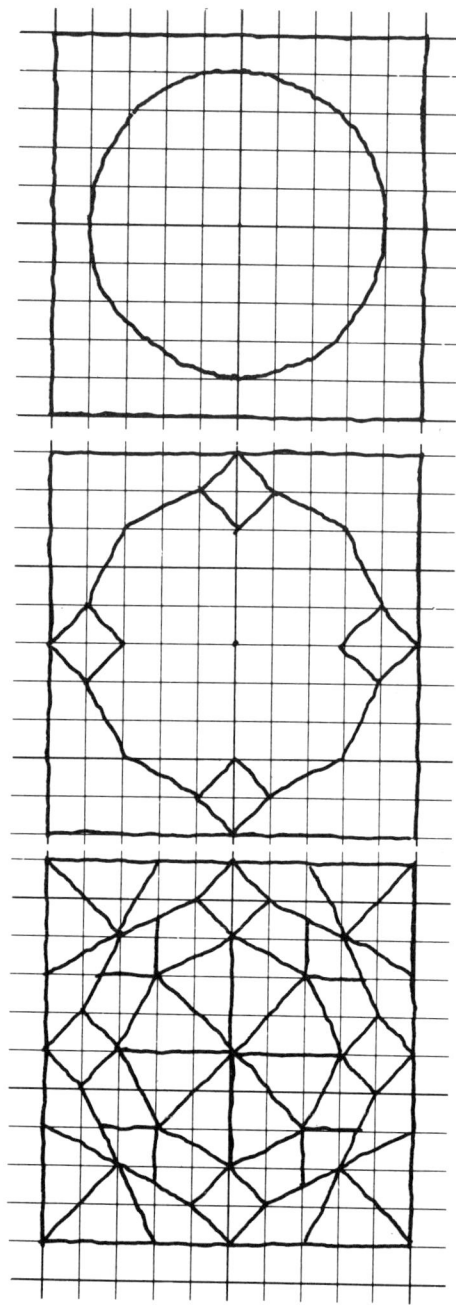

Cushion or Pillow

a. Draw a square, ten squares on a side.

b. Draw a circle inside the square with a radius of four squares.

c. Draw the circle with angular lines around its circumference, using the grid as a guide. If you want to emphasize the center, draw the angles *outside* the compass circle. If, on the other hand, you want to emphasize the corners, make the circle smaller by drawing the angular lines *within* the compass circle.

d. If necessary, draw jagged points and divide the circle into separate parts.

e. Draw in the lines dividing up the corner area, correct any errors (for example, parts that are too small or angles that are too small to sew easily).

f. Enlarge (Technique 6) and stitch. For a pillow about 15 inches (38 cm) square, □ = 6 is suitable.

g. For mounting instructions, see page 78.

Squares

Simple patterns of well-chosen material often look very beautiful. This block of nine squares (nine-patch) in light/dark colors is quickly and easily sewn (Technique 1) and offers many possibilities for compositions.

To streamline the pattern-making process, the pieces can be cut directly from pattern paper. Next, some of the squares can be cut in half diagonally—thus, no drawing and construction work will be necessary. Just follow the technique instructions.

On the next page, some of the many possibilities are sketched out.

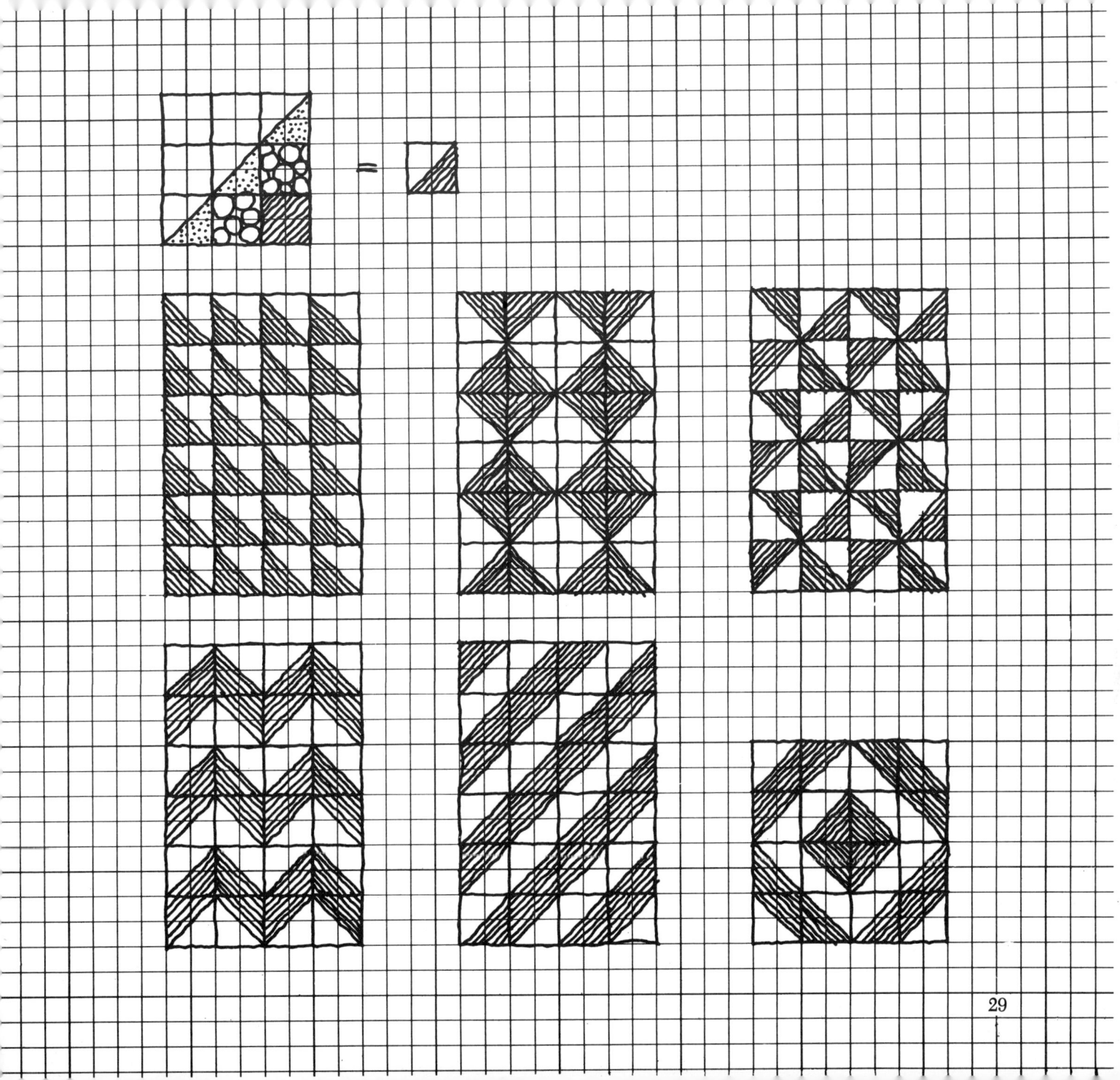

Hearts

In its shape and form, a heart looks harmonious and soothing; it is always with you, whether or not you can see it. In Denmark, it's hard to imagine a Christmas without hearts—big or small, made of glazed paper, appliquéd onto a Christmas tablecloth. In this book, you will find instructions for a Christmas tapestry and an Advent calendar (see page 50 and following), both with heart motifs.

Why not sew hearts in patchwork?

First, outline the heart on graph paper, making sure that the curves are as round as possible. When you have found a harmonious and beautiful outline, split the heart up (see drawing) into handle, curves, and interlaces, if you like. (My hearts resemble spades as often as not.) If you like, divide still further—into many individual parts for big hearts and few parts for small hearts. Enlarge the hearts to a size convenient to work with, and sew together according to the techniques.

Mount the work according to its function (see page 77 and following) and the effect you desire.

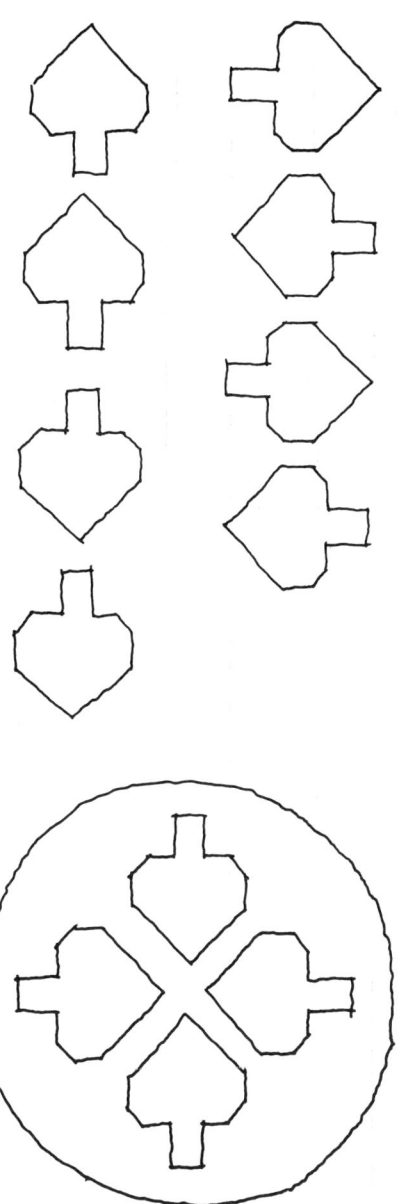

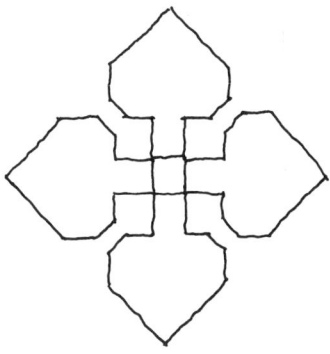

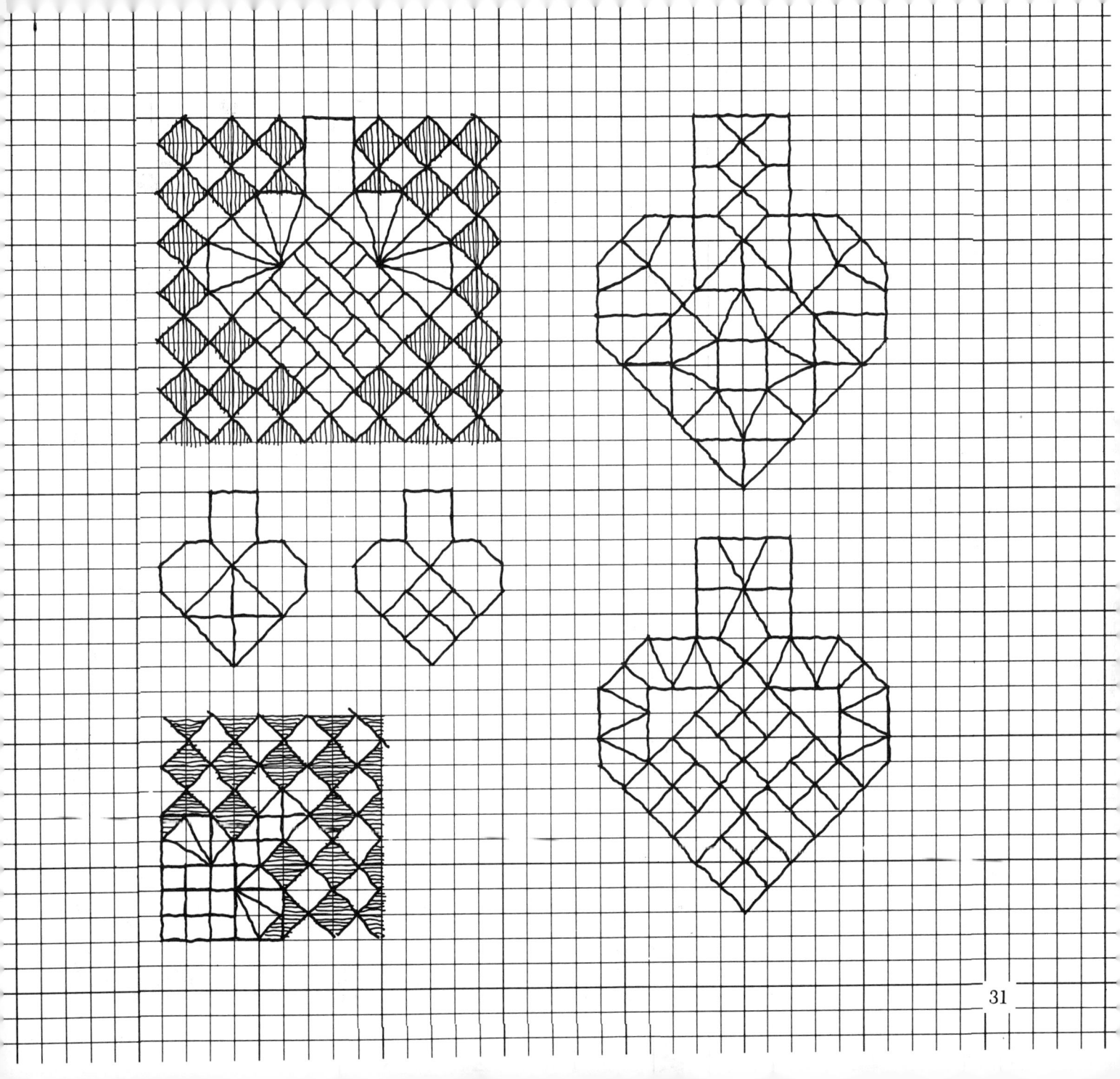

See instructions on
pages 73 and 74.

32

Easter Eggs

Use the squares on graph paper as a guide to draw the outline of an egg, trying to bring out its characteristic form (a pointed and a round end).

Think about why an egg is an egg. You may even find it helpful to write down a few ideas or words that describe or suggest eggs; they may be a help later on when you come to group colors and work out designs.

If it is difficult to draw the egg, try cutting it out in paper first and then drawing the outline on the grid paper.

Straighten the curved lines. Use lines and diagonals over one, two, or three squares.

Divide the egg into smaller parts, using a ruler and sharply pointed pencil. Look at your suggestion words; they may give you an idea for a specific design. Avoid angles that are either too obtuse or too acute. The way an eggshell breaks may suggest natural divisions. If you divide the egg into many parts, it looks larger—fewer parts will make the egg look smaller.

Follow the Techniques when making your Easter eggs. Sew two together to make a wall-hanging (put wrong sides together, then turn right-side-out through an opening you've left along the seam for this purpose, and catch-stitch the seam closed). Or sew many eggs to a table runner (see page 73).

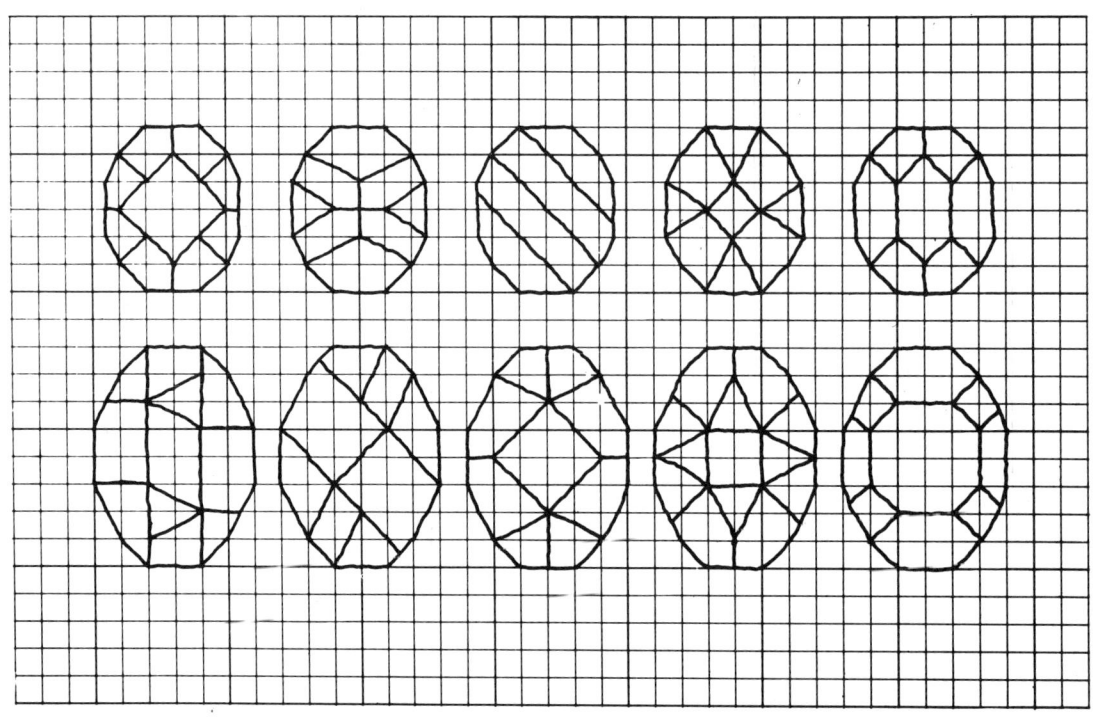

34

Scissors Case

Pattern

Lay your scissors on stiff paper and outline them on the paper. Draw straight lines from point to "ear," (handle) and then between the ears (folding line). Extend the lines until they cross. Make the pattern ¼ inch (6 mm) wider along each of the two long sides. If necessary, round the corners of the point. Draw the flap under the "ears" and overlapping a portion of the front (see diagram).

Note that the flap must extend down well over the front part. Trace over the outline of the flap on another, thinner piece of paper. Cut out the shape and then position it above your scissors case outline, placing fold line on fold line so that the curve is at the top of your shape. Trace onto the stiff paper to make the full paper pattern for the back of the scissors case. The pattern for the front can be made from the same shape after the back lining has been cut. The front pattern is the portion shaded in the diagram. For its top edge, draw a concave curve *above* the line the flap will extend to when it is folded forward. See the dash lines in the diagram. Cut out the back lining. If you plan to use interlining, use the lining pieces as your pattern.

Sewing Instructions:
a. Decorate one side of each piece (Technique 7) with narrow bias or straight strips (if necessary, baste interlining to the lining before doing the patchwork).
b. Edge the upper rim of the front piece with a bias strip. Then stitch the case together with bias strips (quilt *before* stitching together if you use interlining). Run the bias strip or tape up past the back-

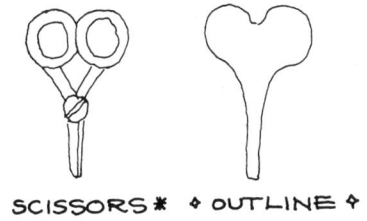

* SCISSORS *   ◆ OUTLINE ◆

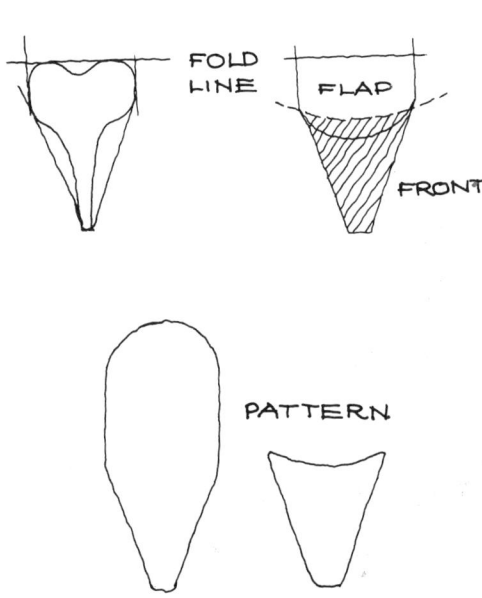

FOLD LINE   FLAP   FRONT

PATTERN

to-front joining, all the way around the front flap. Make the seam as inconspicuous as possible. Finally, mount a press button or a snap fastener. See page 56 for positioning.

See page 60 and following for instructions.

Butterflies

A butterfly—fluttering, graceful, and light—may easily inspire a merry soul to attempt to create this impression in patchwork.

First of all, you must look at a butterfly carefully. Are its wings similar? Where does its body end? How many colors are there in its wings? (It is often easier to read a book on butterflies than to flutter after the butterfly itself; and the book may give the answers to many of your questions.)

Once you have a good idea of what a butterfly looks like to guide you, proceed, following the suggestions for patterns and the instructions below.

Large Butterfly

Draw a butterfly on graph paper; start with the body. Next draw the outline of the wings—use only the squares and the diagonals, and lines at least two squares long (or diagonals covering two squares). Finally, divide the wings into smaller units (Techinques 4 and 5.)

Convert the butterfly into a proper, "sewable," size (Technique 6) and sew, following patchwork Technique 1.

Find a background if the finished butterfly is to be entirely of patchwork.

Small Butterfly

a. Cut a square of paper of about the size you desire—for example, about 7 inches square (18 cm × 18 cm). Fold in half and cut out a simple butterfly, one without too many small curves and lines. Use as much paper as possible, and get close to the edges of your measured paper. If necessary, cut several and choose the best one. (Consult the diagram, to the right.)

b. Put the butterfly on pattern paper and draw its outlines with a pencil.
c. Now use ruler and pencil to make the butterfly into a patchwork butterfly by straightening curved lines. Draw the body with straight lines. Divide the wings into individual pieces. Mark according to Technique 5 and sew following Technique 1.

Suggestions for Application:

See the photographs on page 40.
1. Big, detailed butterflies as window decorations, mounted in a hoop or a wrought-iron ring (see page 70).
2. Big butterfly and background rounded into a tea cozy (see page 69).
3. Butterfly and background square as the center section of a cushion sewn Log-Cabin style (see page 68).
4. Butterflies for placemats or doilies.
5. Butterfly as a flap decoration for a clutch purse (see page 67).
6. Butterfly as apron bib.

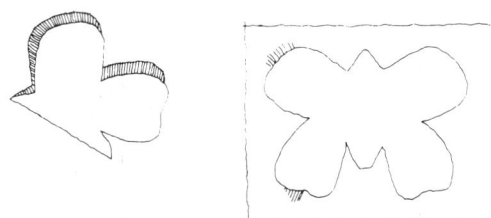

BROWN WRAPPING PAPER

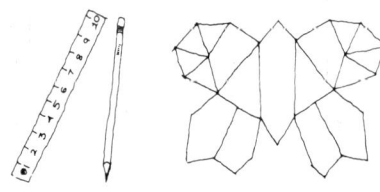

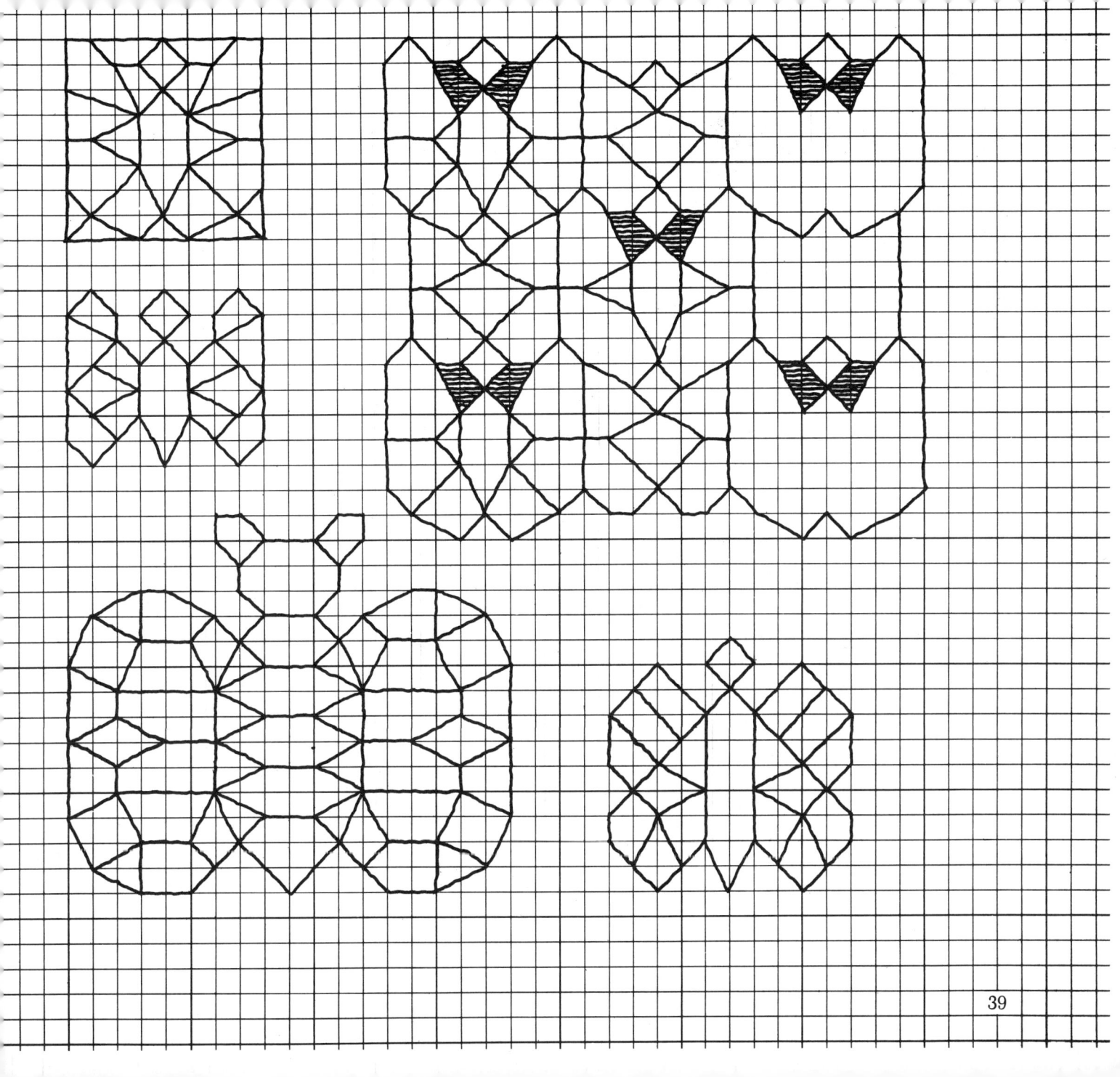

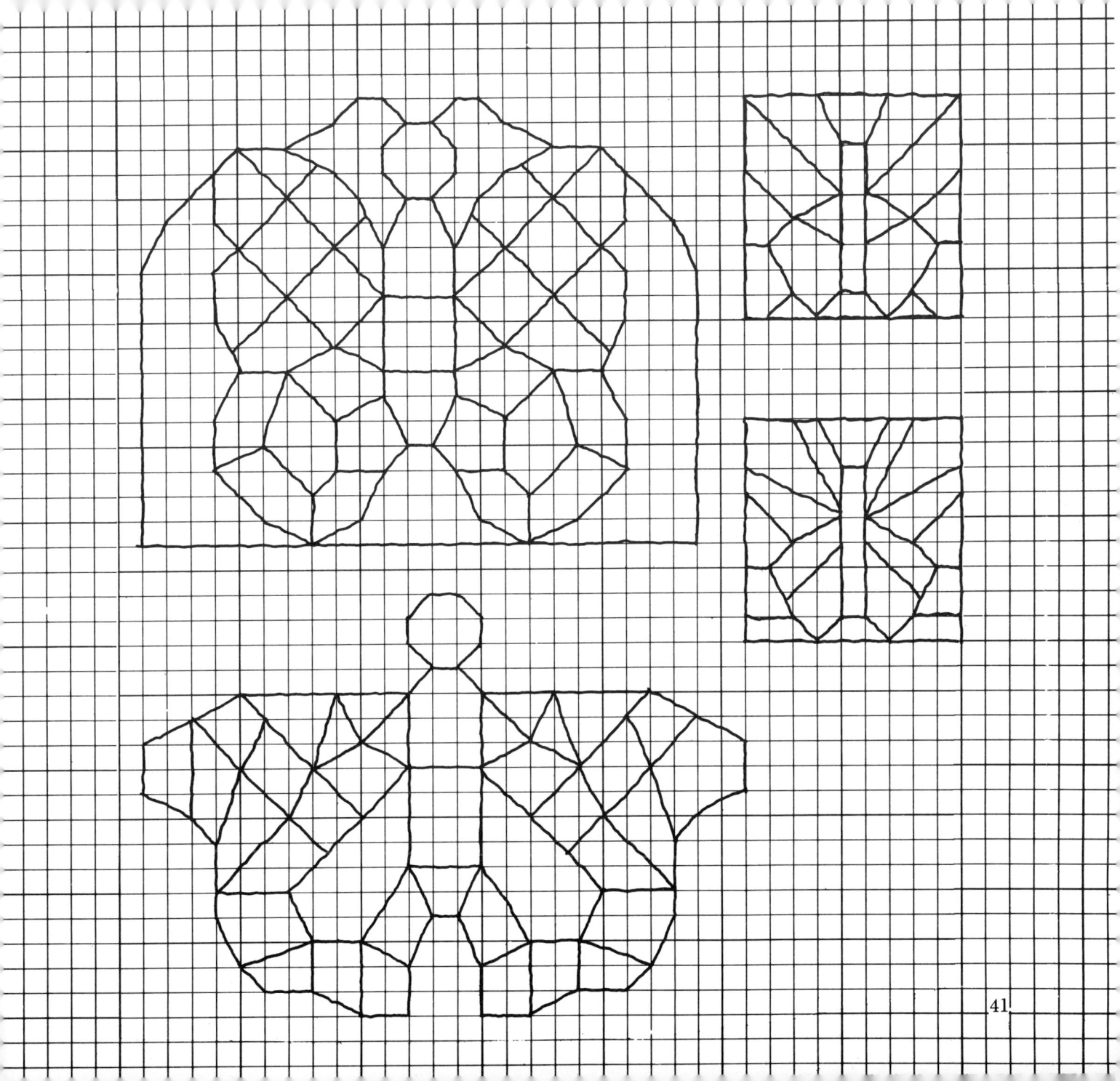

41

About Colors

When spring finally comes, I become so intoxicated and happy that I dig out a lot of brightly colored scraps, because the desire to work with all colors suddenly arises. Throughout our dark, wet winter, I seem carefully to select a few delicately matched colors. But the spring color "explosion" is a question of the rainbow—the whole color wheel!

If you are uncertain of how to handle color or cannot decide what colors you like, try the following patchwork color exercises, which are split up into small tasks but, as a group, give you good practice in combining a range of colors. You can keep your pieces as color samplers or finish them and use them as described. Supplement your knowledge of colors at the library.

Exercise 1: Combi-Star Pillow in Solid Colors

1. Draft a hexagon on gray cardboard (tablet-back or shirt cardboard), using a circle with a radius of about 7 inches (18 cm) and following Technique 2. Cut out.
2. Draw within the hexagon: one hexagon, six triangles, and six diamonds (harlequins). It is easiest to do this by drawing a line from the center of each side of the hexagon to the center of the side two sides away, working clockwise (that is, skipping a side). Mark the sections for color according to the color wheel (see the color key on page 43).
3. Make pattern pieces for each section.
4. Cut material. Then sew the front of the pillow together, using Technique 1.
5. Press, remove the papers, and baste along the outside edges of the pieced hexagon.

6. Estimate the material needed for the back according to the front plus about ⅜-inch (1-cm) seam allowance all around. Fold the seam allowance to the back, pin front and back of the cushion together, and sew on five sides (wrong sides together). Sew close to the edge, and reinforce sewing if necessary. Piping or bias strips may be used to finish the cushion edges, if desired.
7. Fill the pillow well with a foam cushion or polyester fiberfill (about 10½ ounces [300 grams]). Sew the sixth side closed.
8. Cover a large button with material and sew it to the center of the cushion.

Exercise 2: "Color Wheel" in Fancy Materials

1. Draw two circles directly on pattern paper, one with a radius of about 5 inches (13 cm), and another inside it with a radius half of this (2½ inches [6.5 cm]), both with the same center. Construct an octagon inside each circle, and draw lines from the corner of the inside octagon out to the corners of the outside one.
2. Use the primary colors (red, blue, and yellow) in the positions shown in the diagram. Include green as a fourth ground color. Make the pattern pieces and mark them with color designations (Technique 5).
3. Choose materials (fancy fabrics only) with values following the color wheel. For example, an orangey color should go between red and yellow. Cut out the pieces and sew, following Technique 1.
4. Press. You can appliqué the circle onto a tea cozy, for example.

Exercise 3: Gray-Scale Houses

1. Draw a simple and uncomplicated house (or row of houses: see page 44). Cut the individual shapes out of fusible interfacing.
2. Choose material in shades of black through gray to white (there are shades of black and white in fabric as for other colors). Press the interfacing onto the back of the fabrics. Calculate seam allowances and cut. Finally, baste and sew.
3. Decorate the houses if you wish and use them, for example, on the back of a vest or jacket.

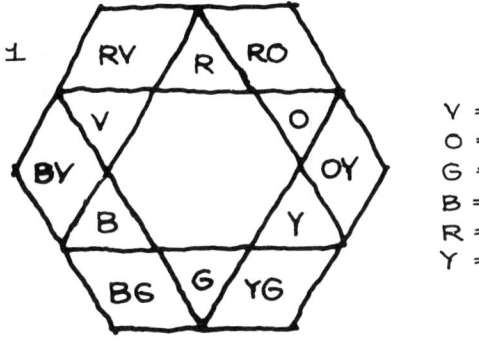

Y = VIOLET
O = ORANGE
G = GREEN
B = BLUE
R = RED
Y = YELLOW

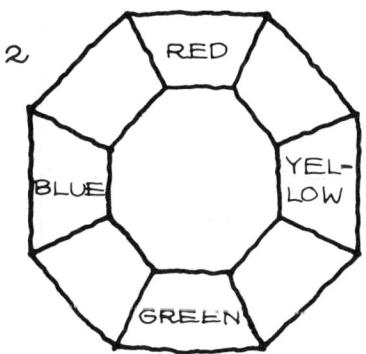

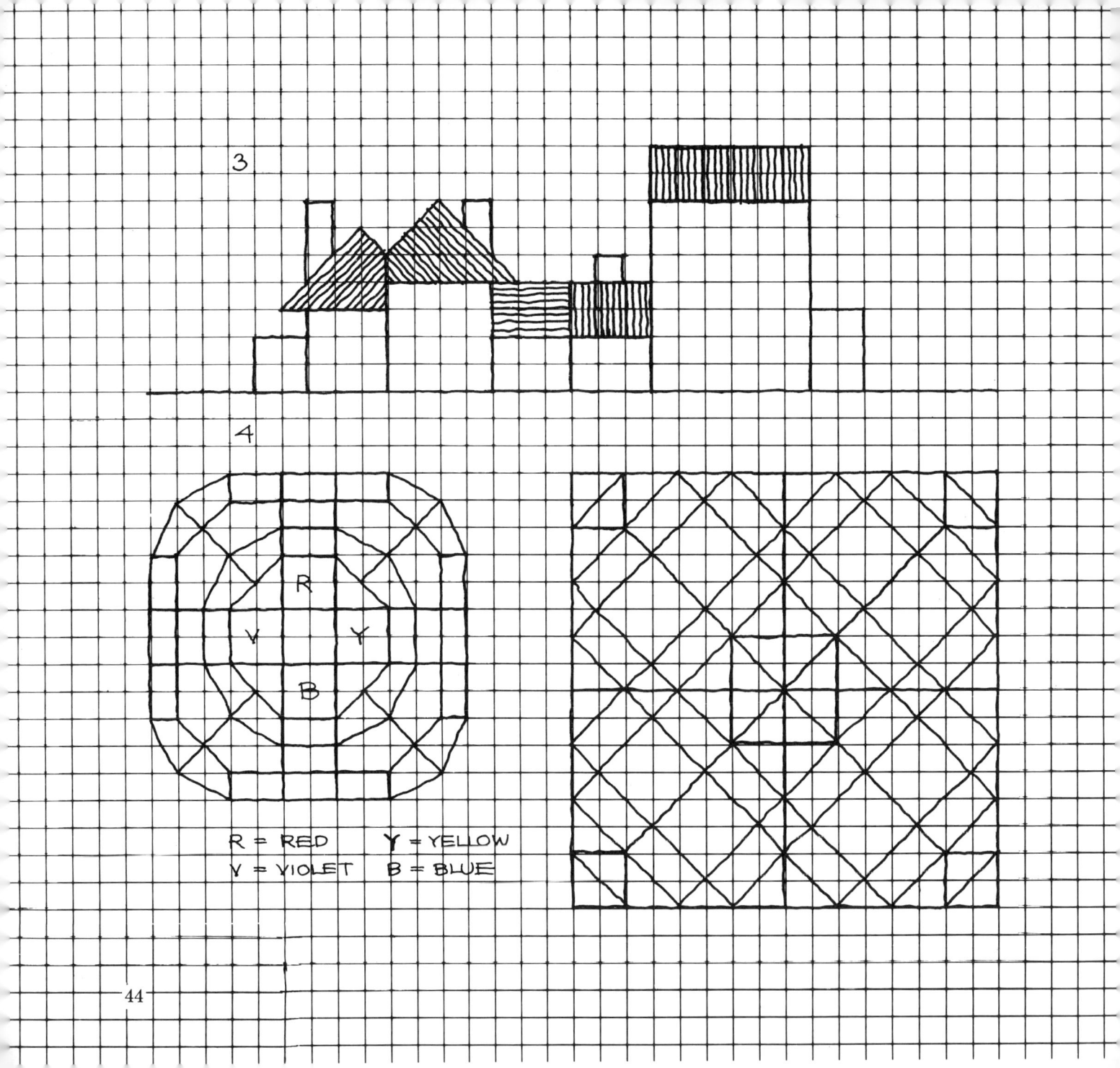

3

4

R = RED   Y = YELLOW
V = VIOLET   B = BLUE

Exercise 4: Spring Tapestry

As a final task, I suggest a small tapestry or wall-hanging called "Spring," in which you should try to include the entire scale of colors on the color wheel. Start, for example, with a geometric shape, such as a hexagon or an octagon. A pattern of your own drawn on pattern paper (see Exercise 1) may also be the starting point. I have graphed some suggestions here and on the facing page. Enlarge your design to the desired size, □ = 4 or □ = 5, for example.

Choose plain as well as fancy materials, light and dark, and plan them so that they flow like the colors on the color wheel. Refer to the techniques as you develop and sew your pattern.

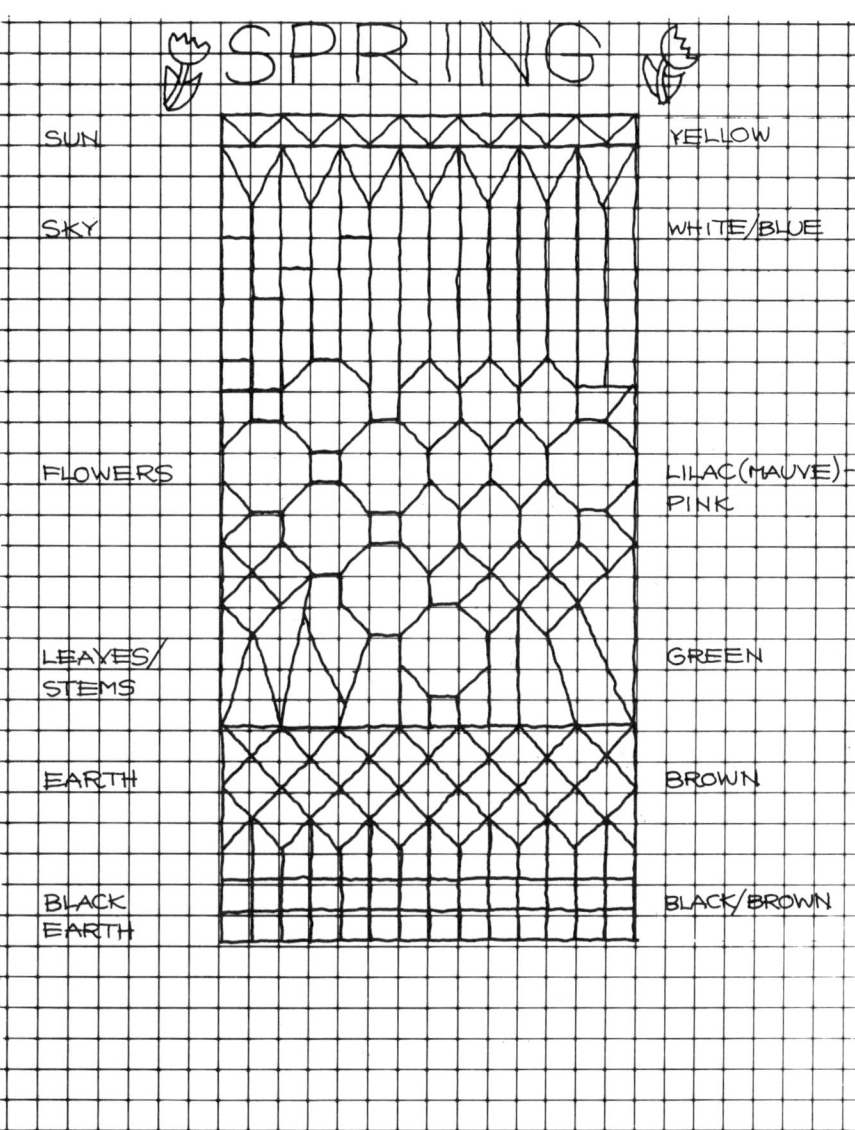

PROJECTS

Handbag

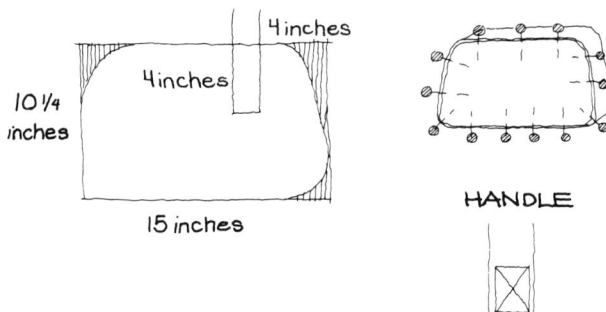

Tuck in and stitch on the handle, as shown.

Materials: 32 inches (80 cm) quilted cotton fabric, 36 inches (1 m) wide. Cotton strips and remnants. 18-inch (45-cm) heavy zipper. Bias strips, about 3½ yards (3 m). Cardboard, 4½ inches × 11 inches (11 cm × 28 cm).
Pattern: Two side panels, 10¼ inches × 15 inches (26 cm × 38.5 cm). Two handles, 3½ inches × 32 inches (9 cm × 80 cm). Two zipper panels, 5 inches × 18 inches (13 cm × 45 cm). One bottom panel, 5 inches × 28¾ inches (13 cm × 73 cm). If desired, an inside pocket: cut two pieces about 8 inches (20.5 cm) long and the width of the side panels. Seam allowance has been included in all these measurements.

Sewing and Finishing Instructions:

a. Cut out two side panels and decorate (following Technique 7, for example). Stay-stitch close to the edges. Finger-press with fingernail or thimble; avoid pressing.

b. Cut two pocket shapes (if a pocket is desired). Right sides together, stitch a seam at the top, turn right-sides-out, and zigzag the pocket to the wrong side of the decorated panel.

c. Cut handles. Stitch a ¼-inch (6-mm) double seam along the edges, turn under ¾ inch (2 cm), and stitch them onto the panels as shown, positioning them about 4 inches (10 cm) from the upper edges and about 4 inches (10 cm) in from the right and left sides of the bag.

d. Cut the top panels and slash lengthwise for the zipper opening. Fold under ⅜ inch (1 cm) and insert the zipper between the two pieces and between front and bottom side of the zipper panel. Baste if necessary and sew. (Use a special zipper foot if you have one). Sew bottom panel and assembled zipper panel together into a 46½-inch (118-cm) ring. Sew an extra line of stitching to secure the joining. Mark the middle of the bottom panel and the middle of the zipper panel.

e. Fasten the side panels to the ring with pins, on both sides and all around, with pins, so that the seam allowance is outside the bag. Stitch all the way around through all thicknesses, ⅜ inch (1 cm) from the edge.

f. Sew edgings or bias borders over the seams.

g. Cut a bottom of heavy tablet-back or shirt cardboard, 4⅓ inches × 11 inches (11 cm × 28 cm). Sew a bag of cotton fabric with one edge left open, insert the cardboard, finish the edge, and stitch the bottom to the bag inside.

Cosmetics Bag—Machine-Sewn

Materials: Cotton remnants, torn in 1⅜-inch (3.5-cm) wide strips. Two pieces of sheeting or other ground cloth material for lining, about 10 inches square (25 cm × 25 cm). Top bar fastener of amber-colored plastic (see drawing), about 4¾ inches (12 cm).

Sewing and Finishing Instructions:

a. Draw a pentagon (Technique 2) on pattern paper with sides about 1½ inches long (4 cm).

b. Trace the pentagon onto sheeting. Using the pentagon as your center, cut out the sides of the bag to about the desired finished size plus seam allowance. Place strips face down and work Log Cabin (Technique 7), beginning on the pencilled lines of the center pentagon. Follow the technique. Sew three rounds.

c. Another, matching pentagon should be sewn next, again with strips. Trim edges.

d. Cut lining, using the trimmed pentagon as your patterns. Right sides together, stitch, then turn right-side-out and zigzag the last side together from the right side (the fastener edge). Repeat for the other pentagon.

e. Stitch the two halves together just inside the edges, as shown. Mount the fastener as instructed by the manufacturer, first at the corners and then along the short sides. Finally, distribute the width evenly as necessary and complete the fastener closing.

Three Pairs of Potholders—
Machine-Sewn

Materials: Preshrunk cotton fabric in strips 1¾ inch (4.5 cm) wide. Six pieces of preshrunk cotton fabric for the backs, about 10 inches square (25 cm × 25 cm). Six pieces of lining or ground cloth, same as back measurement. Six pieces of heavy interlining, such as terry cloth, same as back measurement. Bias strip, about 21 feet (6.6 m), to be cut in six lengths, about 3½ feet (1.1 m) each (do not cut until ready to use).

Sewing and Finishing Instructions:

The potholders consist of a patchwork front (sewn first), interlining, and lining or backing. The whole is quilted, and the potholders are finished with bias strips.

a. Tear, cut, iron material according to Technique 7.

b. Machine-sew patchwork on the background fabric:
two pieces with strips parallel to the side (Technique 7).
two pieces with diagonal strips (Technique 7).
two pieces in squares (Technique 8). If desired, use Log Cabin border.

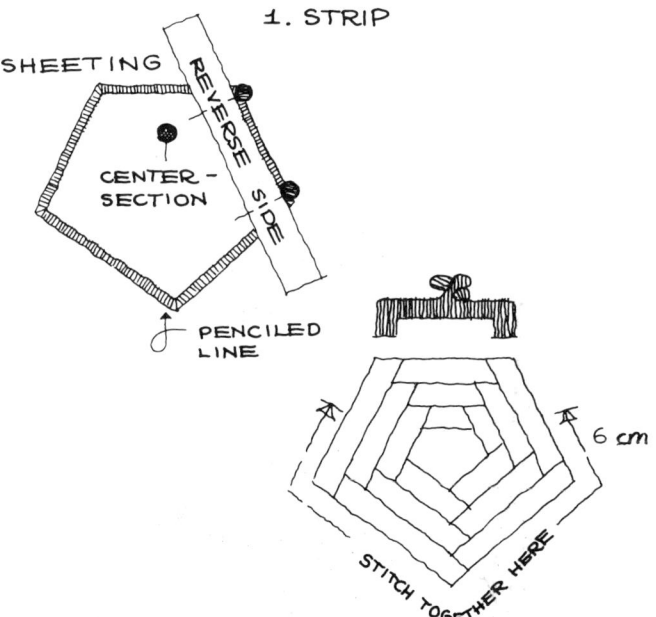

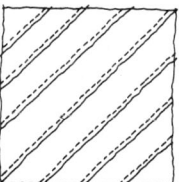
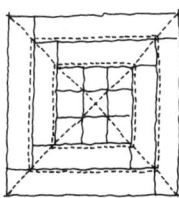

47

c. Quilt (see page 81) the potholders in the design shown by the dash lines in the drawings, zigzag around the outside, and trim edges.

d. Sew a loop to hang the potholder by. Sew the ends of the loop to the edges of one corner of the potholder border (see the diagram). A 5½-inch (14-cm) loop will be ample.

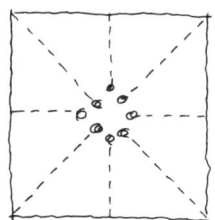 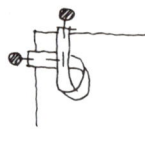

NOTE: The checked potholders are sewn on ground material 8¼ inches square (21 cm), with squares 2⅓ inches (6 cm) on a side.

49

Christmas Tapestry—Handsewn
(Advanced)

Materials: Sixteen sheets of pattern paper. Cotton fabric: red, lilac, light red, and plum colors. Lining fabric, about 3¼ feet (1 m). Batting or interlining, about 3¼ feet (1 m). A rod for hanging.

Final Measurements: About 32 inches × 38 inches (81 cm × 96.5 cm)—longer if you use the design shown to the right.

Sewing and Finishing Instructions:

a. Tape sixteen fresh sheets of pattern paper together accurately (or rule out your own if you can get large sheets or a roll of brown wrapping paper at least 1 yard wide).

b. Enlarge your tapestry design (two possibilities are shown at right) on paper. Here, □ = 8.

c. Choose materials and lay the fabrics out as you like. Mark all parts carefully, for example, hearts with letters, background with numbers (Technique 5). Make the necessary notes (for position or grain, for example).

d. Sew the tapestry together according to Technique 1. If you are not quite confident about your choice of materials, sew the heart first and then choose background fabrics.

e. Press, then remove the pattern papers. Place the tapestry on interlining and lining, and baste the layers together (see page 81). Cut the lining with about ⅜-inch (1-cm) seam allowance; tuck the seam allowance over the interlining, but so that it is not visible behind the patchwork when the piece is seen from the front. Clip acute angles, if necessary to get the tapestry to lie flat, and baste around the perimeter carefully (if desired, mount loops as shown on page 48). Keep checking to be sure that the lining material cannot be seen from the front.

f. Quilt the heart and the background, and, finally, finish the border by top-stitching just inside edge.

The drawing at bottom right is very suitable for a smaller tapestry. Try □ = 4 for a 16-inch × 20-inch (40.5-cm × 51-cm) hanging.

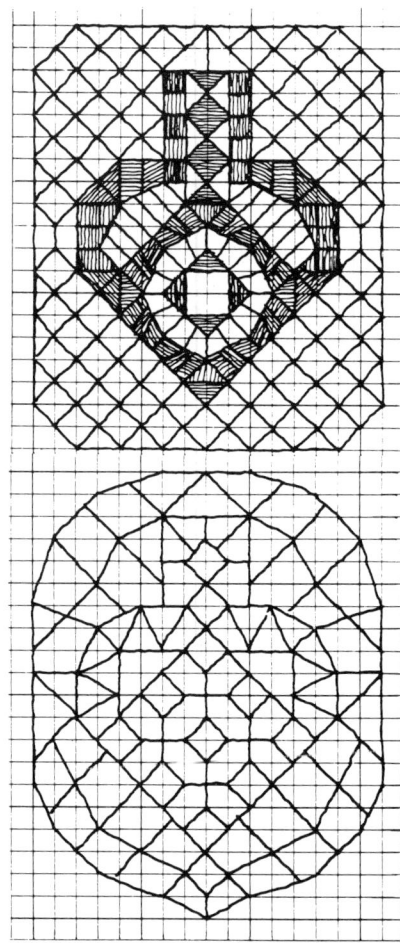

Advent Calendar—Handsewn

Materials: Pattern paper. Cotton fabric in blue, red, and khaki colors. Lining material, about 20 inches × 25¾ inches (50 cm × 65.5 cm). Polyester batting (bonded), about 16 inches × 25 inches (40.6 cm × 63.5 cm). Seven rings. One bell.

Final Measurements: 16 inches × 25 inches (40.6 cm × 63.5 cm).

Sewing and Finishing Instructions:

a. Work out your design on pattern paper (□ = 4, here). I have a heart and the word *Jul*, Danish for "Christmas": my tapestry is used as an "Advent Calendar." Advent calendars, a holiday tradition in Scandanavia, are usually made of paper, with small windows for each of the twenty-four days leading up to Christmas. Each window, when opened day by day, reveals a small present or picture. The presents on my tapestry (see page 52) are meant to be opened one at a time on each of the four Sundays in Advent. The idea can be adapted to any holiday. You may wish to substitute *Yule* or some other word, or just use geometric designs at the top.

b. Choose material. The color photograph on page 52 shows the design in blue-red colors on a khaki background.

c. Mark individual parts carefully with letters and numbers (Technique 5).

d. Sew the calendar together, following Technique 1.

e. Press, and remove pattern papers. Place the calendar on top of batting and lining. Carefully baste all the layers together (avoiding outer edges). Cut the lining with a ⅜-inch (1-cm) seam allowance, and tuck it over the batting or interlining so that it is not visible from the front. Clip curves and sharp angles if necessary. Baste the border carefully (if desired, mount three loops). Keep checking to be sure that the lining cannot be seen from the front.

f. Machine-stitch the border (possibly zigzag), and quilt by hand or machine. Sew on rings (to which you can attach small presents to be opened on certain days leading up to the holiday) and then bell.

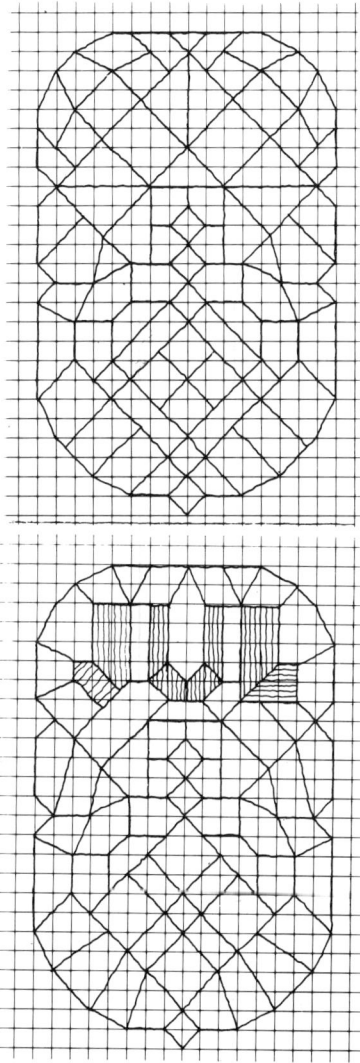

See instructions on following page.

See "About Colors," page 42.

Spanish Carry-All
—Machine-or Handsewn

During a journey to summery sun, I came across this carry-all (though it was in plastic). At all shops and supermarkets, the things being bought were put into these small bags by cashiers and handed over with a smile. This model is very capacious, distributes the weight well, has "hand-minded" handles, and doesn't take up much room when folded.

Cutting Measurements: About 20 inches × 41¾ inches (51 × 106 cm).

Sewing and Finishing Instructions:

a. Choose fabric that is identical on its two sides—reversible or in one color—and not too heavy. Cut out, following the pattern diagram. Note that the bottom of the bag is laid out along the selvage.

b. Fold in a small double (French) seam, as narrow as you can make it, along the scooped openings, and zigzag. Overcast frayed threads center back.

c. Mount any decoration you choose on the center front (use Technique 4, for example).

d. Stitch the bag together along the center back, right sides together. Tack down the seam allowance or fold the raw edges under and top stitch to make a French seam.

e. Press in folds along the dash lines shown on bag and handles. Join raw edges of the handles, front to back.

f. Fold the pleats at the center of the lower edges of the sides so that back and front meet. Stitch the bottom of the bag through all thicknesses, first just inside the edge and then about ⅕ inch (5 mm) in from the edge. Press.

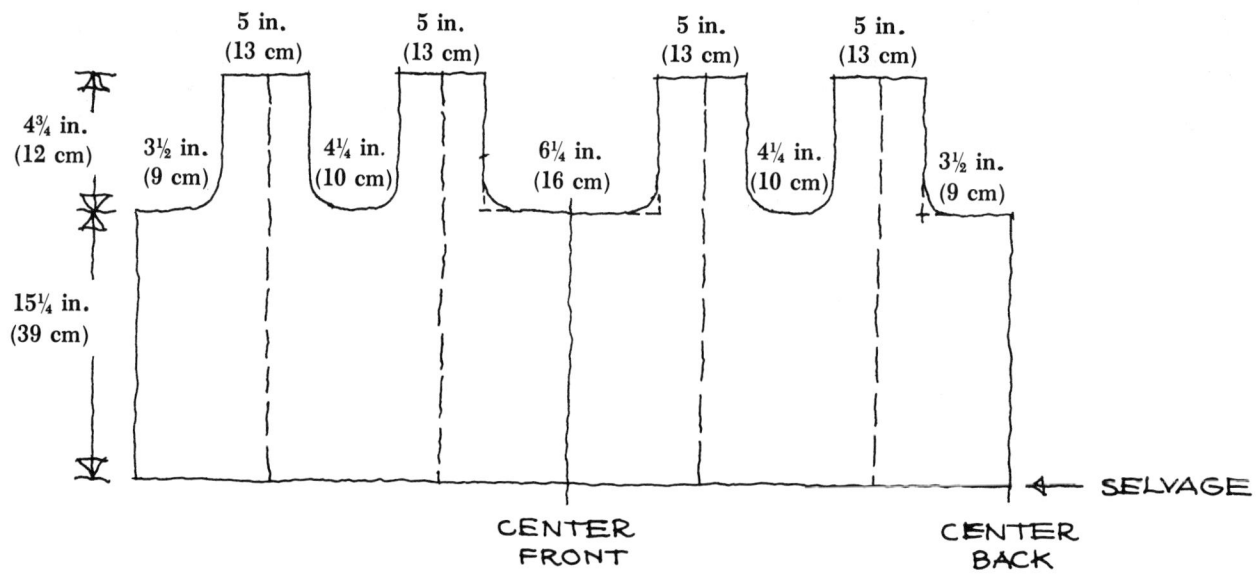

Viking Pillow or Cushion
—Handsewn

Materials: Pattern paper. Cotton fabric remnants or scraps. Backing cloth, about 15¾ inches square (40 cm). A zipper, if desired.

Sewing Instructions:

a. Draw the pattern on pattern paper, following the sketch. The enlargement is □ = 4.

b. Mark the individual parts with letters as shown. As before, the same letter indicates that the same material is to be used. (But G and H may be replaced by E and F, as shown in the photograph at top right on page 56). Also mark the outer edges of all the pattern pieces around the perimeter of the pillow.

c. Cut out the parts; if necessary, use a cork tile or bulletin-board cork covered with fabric to lay out the parts with pins.

d. Cut fabric from the pattern pieces. Add a minimum of ¼ inch (6 mm) for seam allowances.

e. Baste material around pattern pieces, following Technique 1. Be careful at corners, and make sure that the material is tight around the edges. Seam allowances are *not* folded under on marked edges.

f. Press all the individual parts.

g. Line up according to pattern and sew together with small, tight, overcast stitches, as directed in Technique 1. Be careful with the closing stitches.

h. Finish as already described for the first color exercise (see page 42).

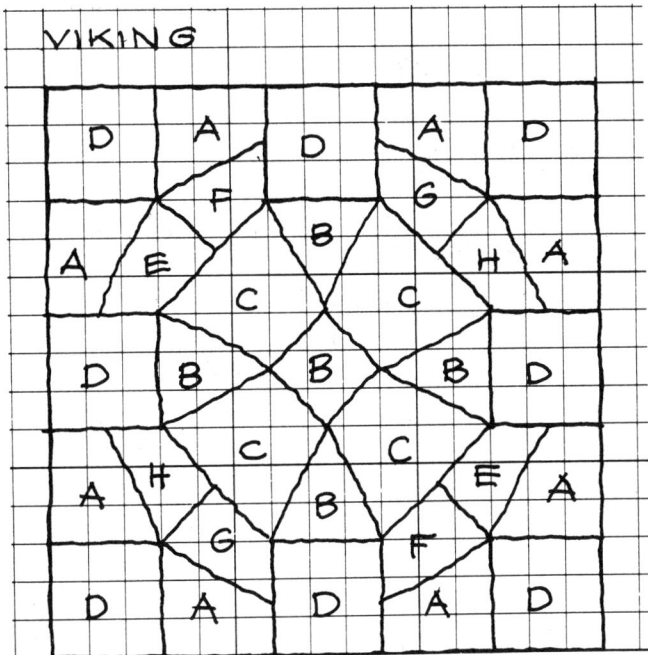

Instructions for scissor case are on page 35.

Viking pillow instructions are on page 55.

56

Patchwork Cushion: "Frame"
—Handsewn

If you have never sewn patchwork before, this cushion is very suitable for beginners. See the color photograph on page 52.

Materials: Pattern paper. Five cotton print remnants or scraps. Backing cloth, about 18¾ inches square (45.75 cm × 45.75 cm). Foam cushion or polyester fiberfill for filling. A zipper, if desired.

Sewing Instructions:

a. Cut twenty 3½-inch × 3½-inch (9-cm × 9-cm) squares; twelve 3½-inch × 3½-inch (9-cm × 9-cm) squares (which are then bisected diagonally to make triangles); and a 6½-inch × 6½-inch (16.5-cm × 16.5-cm) square for the center. The enlargement here is □ = 4; □ = 1 inch (2.5 cm).

b. Put the pattern pieces in front of you on a table. Look at the pattern sketch, and mark with letters designating the fabrics. As usual, the same letter indicates that the same fabric is to be used. I have used B for the center square (M, middle). If your fabrics have an obvious one-way design, indicate this with an arrow showing the direction. Mark the edges that fall along the outside edge of the sketch with a wavy line.

c. Cut material, following the marked patterns and being sure that the one-way designs in your cotton prints are running the way you want them to. Allow about ¼ inch (6 mm) for seam allowances.

d. Baste material around the pattern pieces. Be careful at corners and make sure that the material is tight around the edge of the pattern piece (Technique 1). You'll find more about basting on page 84.

e. Press all units so that the edges are all sharp—this will help your stitching later.

f. Lay out pieces according to pattern and sew together as for Technique 1. Be careful with the closing stitches.

g. Press the entire cushion front, then carefully remove the basting stitches. Finally, remove pattern papers. If necessary, press once more and mount the cushion (see page 78).

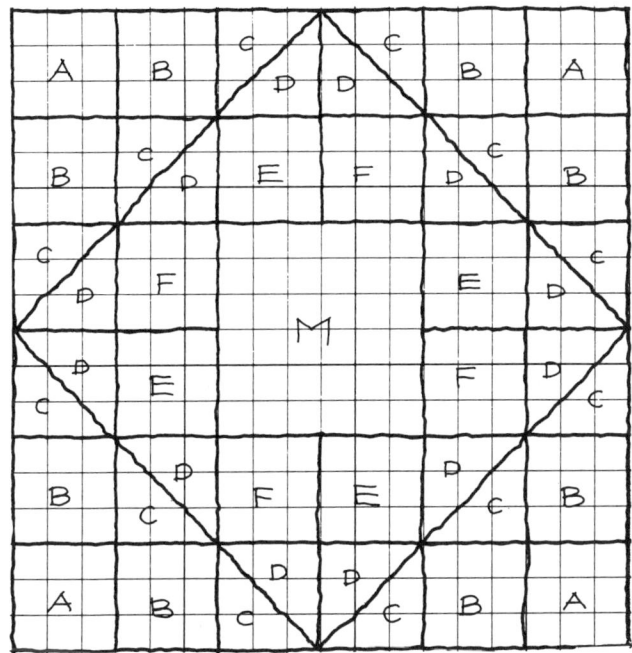

FRAME

Patchwork Cushion: "Diagonal"
—Handsewn

Materials: Pattern paper. Four cotton print remnants or scraps. Backing cloth, about 18¾ inches square (47.6 cm × 47.6 cm). Foam cushion or polyester fiberfill for filling. A zipper, if desired.

Final Measurements: About 18 inches (45.75 cm) square.

Sewing Instructions:

a. Draw an 18-inch (42-cm) square on pattern paper. Using a ruler and sharply pointed pencil, divide each side into thirds and mark each with a point (they will be about 6 inches (15.25 cm) apart). Then draw the diagonals, following the sketch, which is drawn ☐ = 4.

b. Cut out the parts exactly, and mark with letters according to the sketch; again, the same letter indicates that the same material is to be used. Mark the outer edges.

c. Cut material. Add ¼ inch (6 mm) all round for seam allowances.

d. Baste the material around the pattern papers. See Technique 1 and the information about basting on page 84.

e. Press all units so that the edges are sharp. This will make your stitching easier later.

f. Arrange all the pieces according to the sketch and sew together (Technique 1).

g. Press the whole piece, then remove your basting stitches and pattern papers. If necessary, press again. For finishing instructions, see page 78.

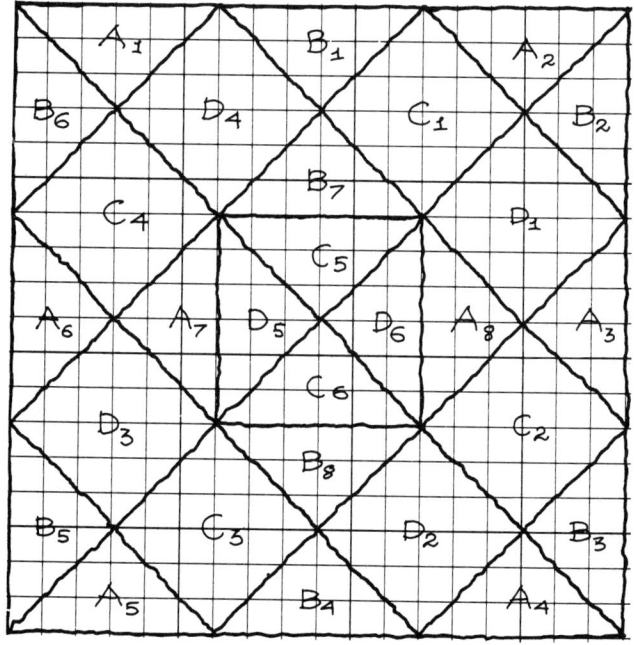

DIAGONAL

Chair Cushion—Machine-Sewn

This cushion is machine-sewn using an old technique related to Log Cabin.

Materials: Cotton fabric in 1¾-inch (4.5-cm) wide strips. Backing or ground cloth, about 15-inches square (38 cm). Lining material, same measurements as for backing. Foam cushion or polyester fiberfill. A zipper, if desired.

Final Measurements: About 13¾ inches square (35 × 35 cm).

Sewing Instructions:

a. Tear, cut, and iron the material as described in Technique 8.

b. Sew patchwork by machine (Techniques 8 and 9) as follows: First, construct the center section with 1¼-inch (3.25-cm × 3.25-cm) squares (cutting size 1¾ inches [4.5 cm] square), alternating colors as shown in the pattern sketch. Use this "nine-patch" as a starting point for the ground material. Looking at the strip diagram, construct the strips: each is a bar the length of the preceding strip. Strips 4 and 5, 8, and 9, and 12 and 13 have a 1¾-inch (4.5-cm) square at each end (finished to 1¼ inches [3.25 cm] square). Add strips in the order shown in the pattern sketch. Finish with one round of solid color as a border.

c. Stay-stitch the cushion front just inside raw outer edges. Trim raw edges and press if necessary.

d. Finish the cushion, with a "peekaboo" border and zipper, for example. See page 78, step 3 and following.

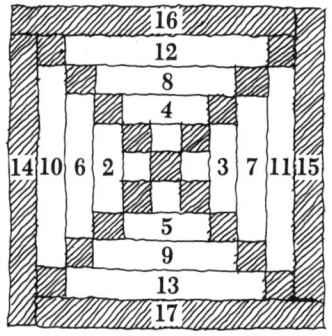

= SOLID COLOR MATERIAL

THE CENTER SECTION IS SEWN FIRST

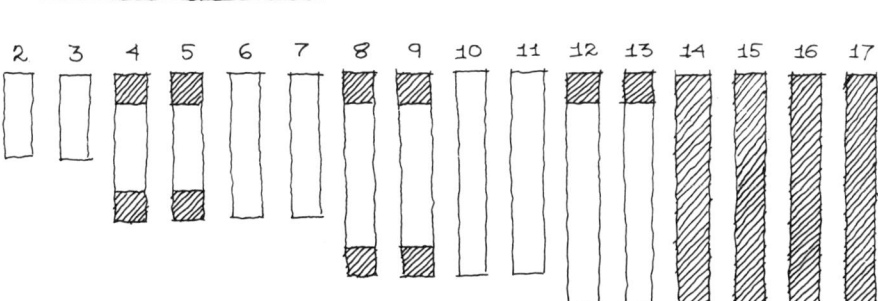

Christmas Cornets—Handsewn

There are many uses for these sprightly holiday decorations, some of which are shown on page 37. Make the cornets larger or smaller as desired for different purposes. This pattern is for cones about 6 inches (15 cm) high.

Materials: Cotton fabric. Lining fabric. Golden decoration braids for trim, about 14 inches (36 cm). Ribbon for handles, about 10 inches (25.5 cm).

Sewing and Finishing Instructions:

a. Design your pattern directly on pattern paper, as follows: draw two circles with the same center, one with a radius of about 6 inches (15 cm) and the other with a radius of about 3½ inches (9 cm). Construct a hexagon within the smaller circle and divide the angles (Technique 2, as shown in the pattern sketches: top and bottom show two possibilities. Cut the circle into thirds, separate pieces for each cornet. Before continuing, cut out the lining for each. Set aside.

b. Working with the cones one at a time, choose material, mark the individual parts, and cut them out. You need not use two pieces for the base of the cone or for portions of the edge decorations. Cut at the arrows or not, as you wish.

c. Sew together, following patchwork Technique 1. Press, and remove pattern papers.

d. Baste golden decoration trim at the top. Right sides together, sew the side seam or seams of the cone. Construct the lining cone. Insert into the first cone, wrong sides together. Position the ribbon handle on the cornet middle. Baste to front. Turn raw edges under so that the lining does not show from the front above braid trim. Pin or baste.

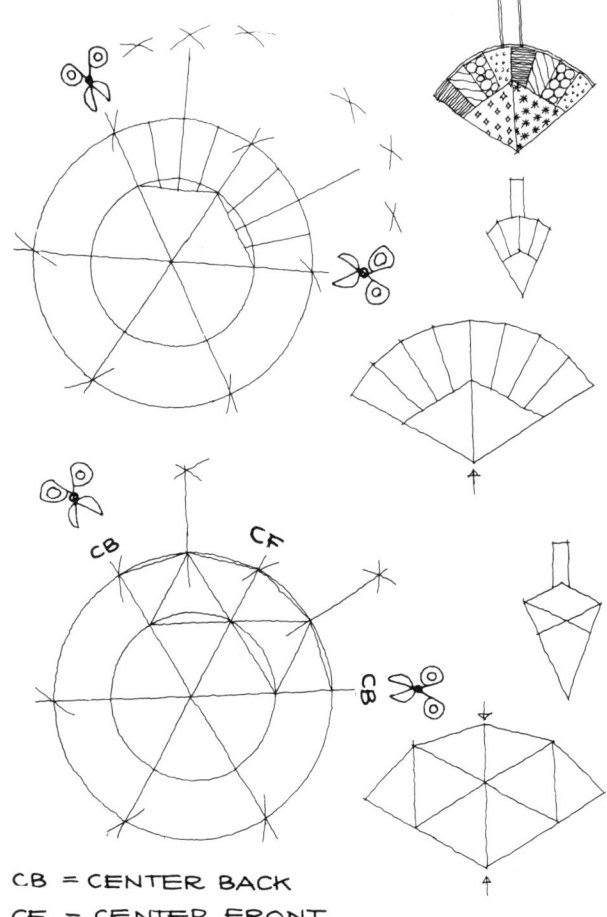

CB = CENTER BACK
CF = CENTER FRONT

e. Zigzag the cornet together from the right side (wide, open zigzag).

Make other cornets in the same way. Fill with Christmas treats or evergreens.

Christmas Star—Machine-Sewn

Materials: Pattern paper. Various fabrics with a golden, soft, or metallic sheen; yellow or coordinating cotton fabric. Thin wire (small star); cardboard tube (larger star). Metal buttons or beads. Foam cushion or polyester fiberfill.

Final Measurements: Large star: 12 inches (30 cm) diameter. Small Star: 9 inches (23 cm) diameter.

Sewing and Finishing Instructions:

a. Draw the pattern (see the sketch on page 64) on pattern paper: one for the front and one for the back. On four-to-the-inch graph paper, for the large star, □ = 4. For the small star, □ = 3.

b. Mark the individual parts (Technique 5). Choose fabric.

c. Cut and sew, following Technique 1. If necessary, use tape to secure seam allowances (for example, if lamé is used). Press only if you are using cotton.

d. Machine-stitch front and back together, except for one of the large points.

e. For both large and small stars, insert thin wire along the inside edge, as shown in the diagram below. The wire should be long enough to use to hang or mount the small star.

f. Fill the star with foam padding, and finish mounting as follows: Large star: Press the cardboard tube (the cardboard tube inside waxed paper or something similar works fine) up into the middle of the star. Cut the tube to fit the star's open lower point; add more foam if necessary; bend the wire ends *up* into the tube; and sew the side together with small stitches, so that the tube is secured. Tuck the seam allowance into the tube, and glue down with rubber cement. Small star: Baste the point together so that the ends of the wire protrude from the corner seam. Twist a spiral for fastening the star.

g. If desired, sew on gold or silver buttons or beads as shown in the color photograph on page 37. Sew on both sides.

The large star can be mounted on top of the Christmas tree; the small one is secured with wire.

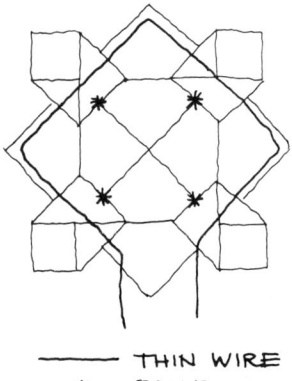

THIN WIRE
* BEAD

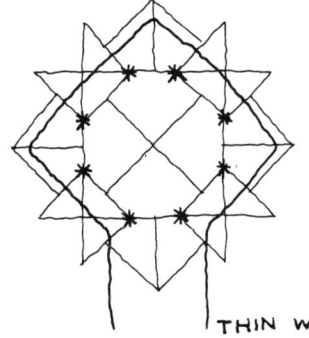

THIN WIRE

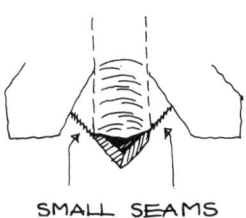

SMALL SEAMS

SEE DIAGRAM PAGE 64.

Christmas Placemats—Handsewn
(or Machine-Sewn and Handsewn)

Materials: Pattern paper. Cotton fabric for placemat, about 15 inches × 21⅔ inches (38 × 55 cm), plain or reversible. Cotton fabric for cornet. Bias binding, 6½ feet (2 m).

Final Measurements: About 14 inches × 20½ inches (36 × 52 cm).

Sewing and Finishing Instructions:

a. Draw a cornet (see page 60) □ = 2 on four-to-the-inch pattern paper (page 63) and sew, following Technique 1. Stay-stitch the edges, including the handle edges.

b. Cut lining with ⅜-inch (1-cm) seam allowance as shown; clip corners, tuck the raw edges under, and zigzag the front and lining together along top edge and sides of handle.

c. Trim the lining on the rest of the cornet so that it is not visible from the front. Position the cornet on the placemat fabric and zigzag it directly to the placemat piece along sides and handle. Be sure that the zigzag is wide enough to catch the free edges of the lining.

d. Make bias binding strips (Technique 10) and use them to finish the placemat edges. Press.

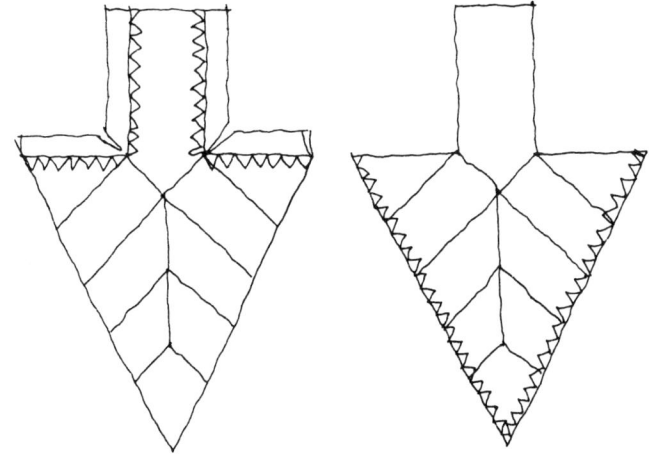

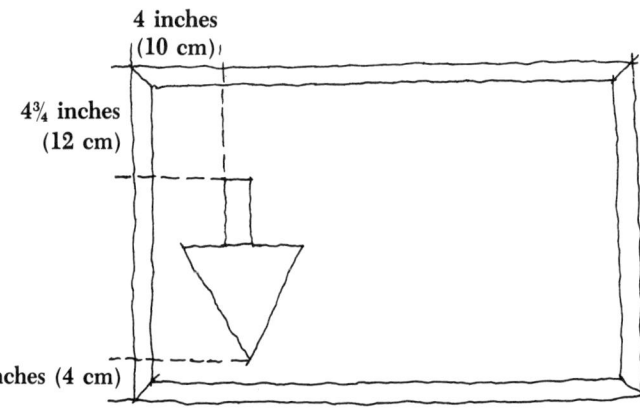

4 inches
(10 cm)

4¾ inches
(12 cm)

1½ inches (4 cm)

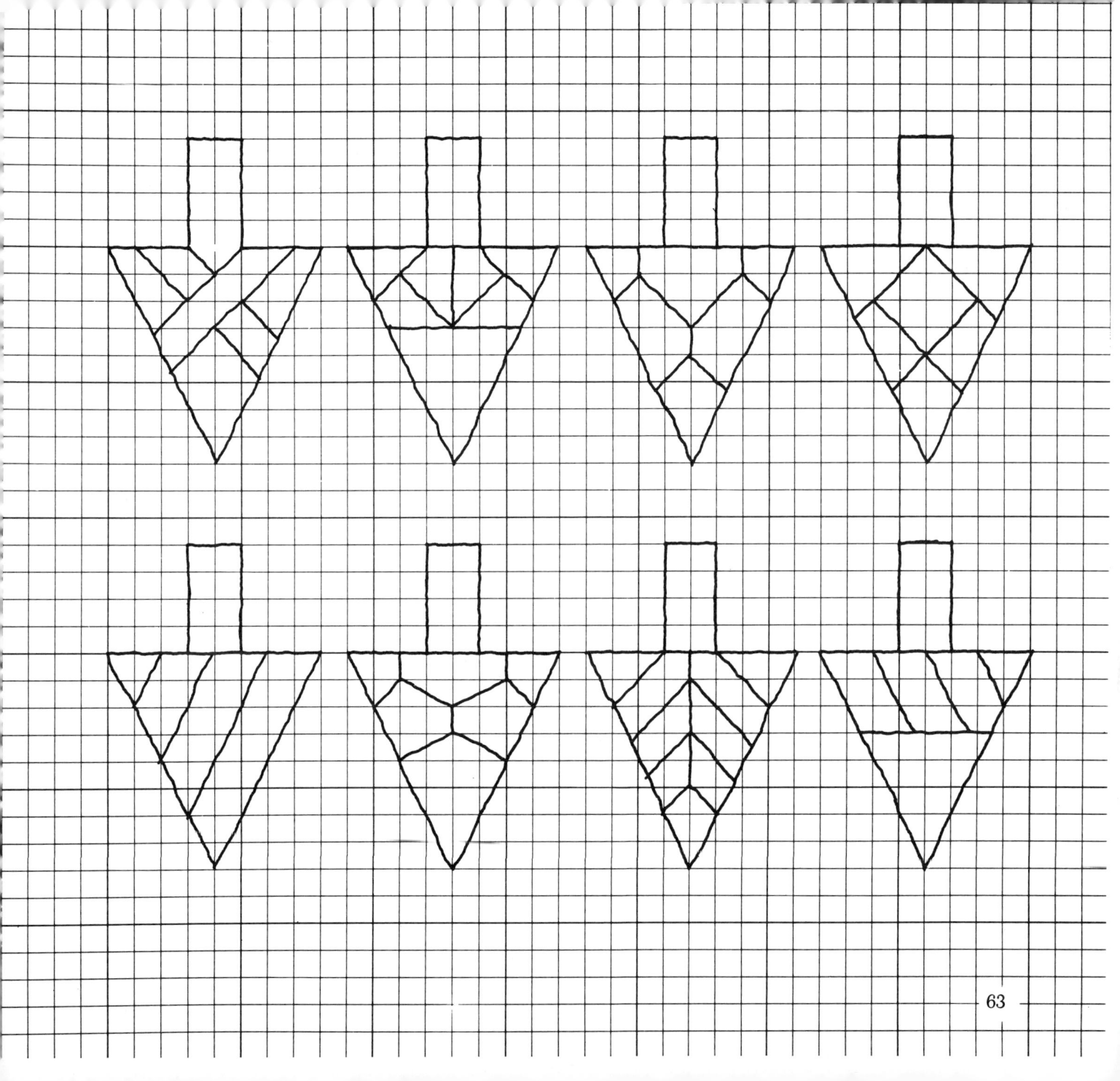

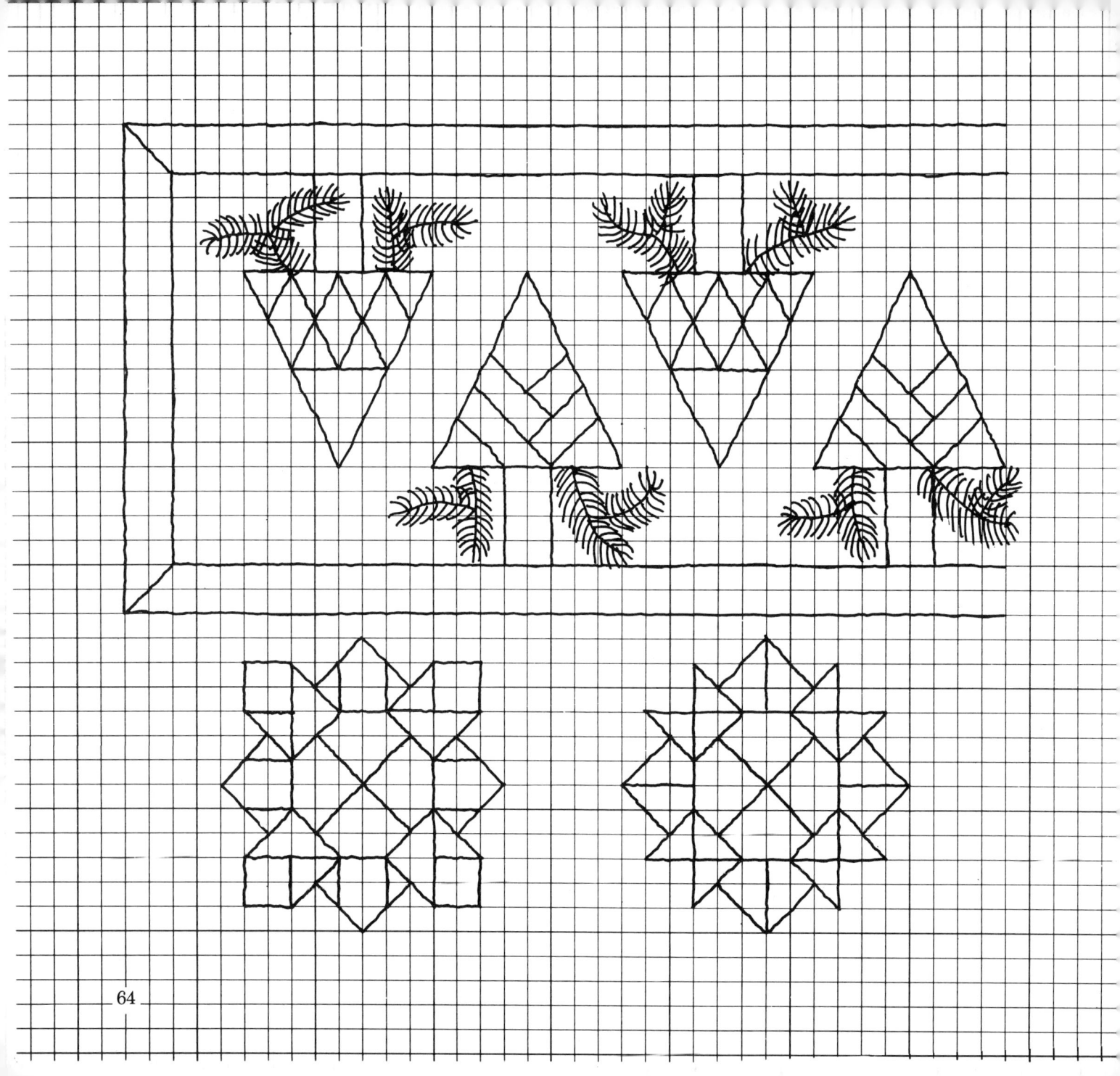

Christmas Runner with Cornets
—Handsewn (or Machine-Sewn
and Handsewn)

Materials: Pattern paper. Cotton fabric (prequilted, if you wish) for runner, 13¾ inches × 43⅓ inches (34 × 110 cm). Cotton fabric for cornets. Bias binding, about 10 feet (3 m).

Sewing and Finishing Instructions:

a. Draw seven cornets (see page 60) on pattern paper, □ = 2 on four-to-the-inch pattern paper.

b. Choose material and mark the individual parts (Technique 5).

c. Cut and sew, using Technique 1. Stay-stitch edges. Press, and remove pattern papers.

d. If you want to be able to fill the cornets with srpuce twigs, and so forth, the cones must be lined. Cut seven linings from the whole cornet pattern, with a ⅜-inch (1-cm) seam allowance along handles and top edge. Clip seam allowance at corners. Tuck seam allowance under and zigzag as shown. The lining on the lower edges is left free.

e. To finish the runner, sew on a bias binding about 1 inch (25 mm) wide: turn under ⅜ inch (1cm) on the right side of the runner, mount the binding as described on page 82, and stitch it to the outer edge.

f. Distribute the cornets, baste them on or secure with pins, and insert the handles underneath the inner edge of the binding. Machine-stitch the inner edge all around.

g. Zigzag the cornets onto the runner (around the lower edges and point only), being certain the stitch is wide enough to catch the free edge of the lining. Press.

h. Put juniper, spruce, holly, or whatever, into the cornets.

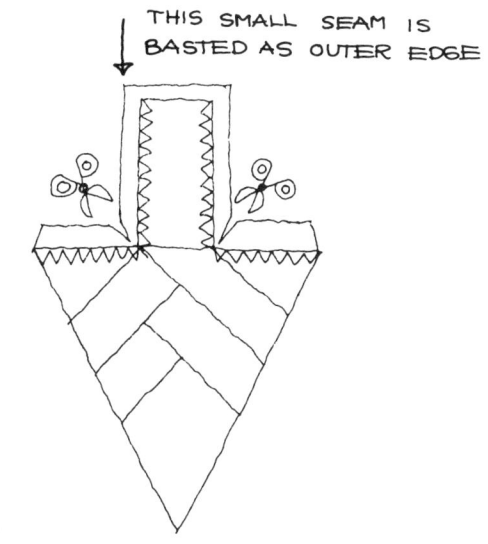

THIS SMALL SEAM IS BASTED AS OUTER EDGE

THE ENTIRE BIAS BINDING MUST BE VISIBLE ON THE RIGHT SIDE.

LOOK AT <u>CORNERS</u> AT THE BACK OF THE BOOK.

Ball—Handsewn

Materials: Cardboard (tablet-back or shirt cardboard). Pattern paper. Cotton fabric, preferably heavy: solids and prints, as described below. Coarse stuffing (the kind used by upholsterers), about 3½ pounds (1.5 kilos).

Final Measurements: 14¼ inches (36 cm) diameter.

Sewing and Finishing Instructions:

a. Draw a pentagon (Technique 2) on cardboard with sides equal to 2¾ inches (7 cm). Cut out. On pattern paper, draw twelve pentagons from the pattern and cut out.

b. Draw a hexagon (Technique 2) on cardboard with a radius of 2¾ inches (7 cm). Cut out. On pattern paper, draw twenty hexagons and cut out.

c. Baste solid material around all pentagons, and printed material around the hexagons, using five prints in the same color family if possible. Press them all.

d. Sew (Technique 1) two flowers composed of a pentagon in the middle and ten hexagons around its sides, as shown in the diagram. Use all five prints around the pentagons. If necessary, sew with doubled thread for greater strength.

e. Sew pentagons in the spaces between the hexagons (see arrows) on both flowers.

f. Sew the two flowers together to make a ball—if necessary, remove the pattern papers—until there are only a few edges left open.

Fill the ball with stuffing, and sew remaining seams.

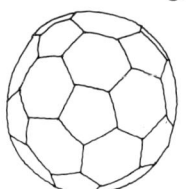 

Brush Case—Machine-Sewn

Materials: Cotton fabric. Interlining. Bias strips, about 29½ inches (75 cm).

Sewing and Finishing Instructions:

a. Cut lining according to your brush measurements; when finished, the case must be somewhat tight. Sample measurements are given in the diagram.

b. Baste on the interlining. Decorate the front, using Technique 7, for example. (Look at the color photograph on page 56.)

c. Edge with bias strips on three sides (see diagram).

d. Fold and zigzag the front of the case together. The stitch must catch the bound edges on both sides. Finger-press the seam flat.

e. Turn the case wrong-side-out and stitch the bottom ⅜ inch (1 cm) from the edge. Turn right-side-out again.

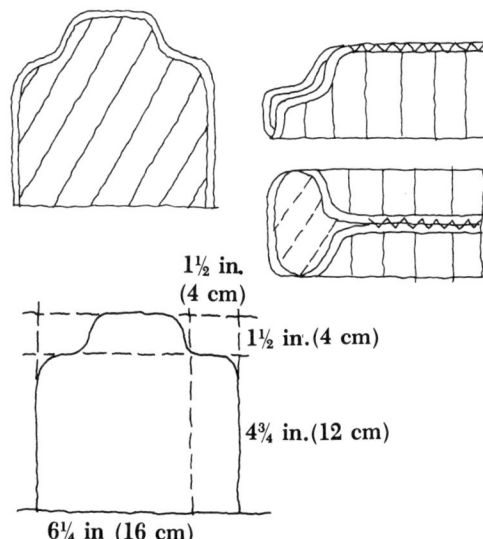

1½ in. (4 cm)

1½ in.(4 cm)

4¾ in.(12 cm)

6¼ in (16 cm)

Clutch Purse with Butterfly Flap
—Handsewn and Machine-Sewn

The clutch purse is sewn of one piece of velvet, with an outside pocket at the back. The flap decoration is sewn by hand. Look closely at the color photograph on page 40 and at the diagram before beginning.

Materials: Pattern paper. Velvet, 13¾ inches × 59 inches (35 × 150 cm). Velvet remnants or scraps for the butterfly. Terry cloth for interlining. Bonded polyester batting. One large snap fastener.

Sewing and Finishing Instructions:

a. Draw the butterfly on pattern paper; □ = 3 (see diagram below). Sew it together, following Technique 1. Note that the clutch purse material is used for the head of the butterfly. Velvet marks easily and will show where you've removed stitches, so work carefully. Baste the seam allowances to the pattern papers without coming through to the front.

b. Cut out the clutch purse to the dimensions in the diagram. Cut terry cloth (or other interlining to stiffen the purse a little) according to the same pattern, and baste it onto the velvet in the seam allowances.

c. Place B against C (right sides together), and stitch ¼ inch (6 mm) from the edge. Place E against D (right sides together) and stitch ¼ inch (6 mm) from the edge. Turn both pieces right-side-out. If

necessary, baste the edges and press on the wrong side, lightly.

d. Fold the sewn pieces carefully right sides together to make them as thin as possible. Place A against F and stitch ¼ inch (6 mm) from the edge on F (it is somewhat difficult, but it can be done). Turn right-side-out; if necessary, stitch the edge of the purse.

e. Mount the butterfly on the flap, folding under the edges ⅜ inch (1 cm) from the outline of the butterfly; if necessary, baste before stitching. Stuff lightly from the top with batting. Quilt (see page 84) and hand-sew the final small seams at the head with blind stitches.

f. Fold one pocket and fold tucks in either side, so that the edges are flush. Fold the other "pocket" back and up. Make tucks in either side so that the edges are flush. Fasten with pins, or baste and stitch all the layers together by machine.

g. Sew on a heavy snap fastener for the closing.

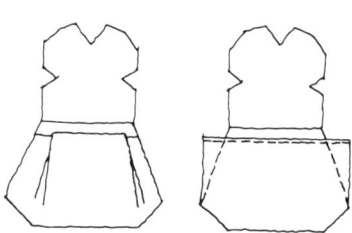

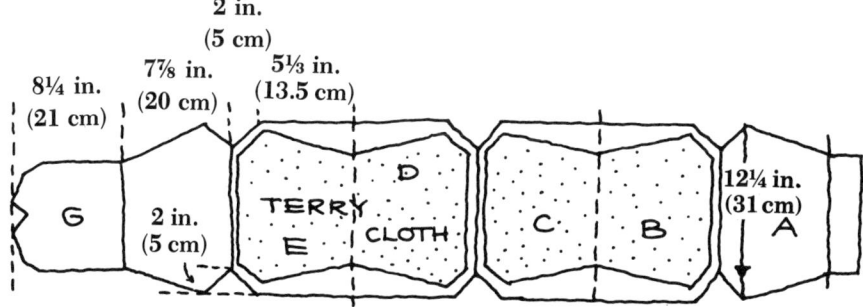

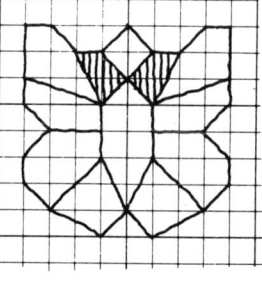

2 in.
(5 cm)

8¼ in.
(21 cm)

7⅞ in.
(20 cm)

5⅓ in.
(13.5 cm)

G   2 in.
(5 cm)

TERRY
E   CLOTH

D

C   B

12¼ in.
(31 cm)

A

Lawn Chair Cushions—Handsewn and Machine-Sewn

The center of this cushion is hand-made; the rest is machine-made for durability. The cushion back has an overlapped closing, so that the cover may easily be removed and washed.

Materials: Pattern paper. Backing cloth, 16¾ inches square (42.5 × 42.5 cm). Cotton prints for butterfly; contrasting but coordinated cotton fabric for Log Cabin; cotton fabric for mounting 16 inches × 23 inches (40.5 × 58.5 cm). Bonded polyester batting, 9 inches square (23 cm) for butterfly. Mat or pad for filling.

Final Measurements: About 16 inches square (40.5 cm).

Sewing and Finishing Instructions:
a. Draw the butterfly on four-to-the-inch pattern paper, □ = 4.
b. Mark the individual parts and cut out paper patterns (Technique 1).
c. Choose fabric. Cut out fabric and sew butterfly, following Technique 1. If you want to baste by machine, see page 84.
d. Press, and remove pattern paper. Mount the butterfly on the backing as the center section of the Log Cabin, basting it over a layer of batting. Finish the cushion following Technique 9 (Log Cabin), with four rounds of 1¾-inch (4.5-cm) (cutting size 2¼ inches [5.75 cm]) strips. Choose a main color and use it for two rounds (preferably the first and last). Make one round in a very light or very dark color.
e. Quilt the butterfly and/or the background.
f. Mount the cushion with an overlapped closing—see page 79.

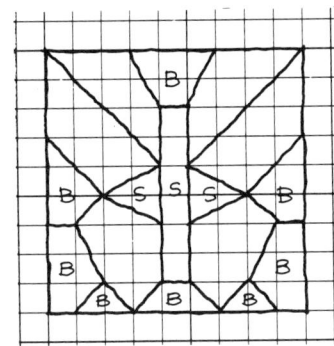

B = BACKGROUND MATERIAL
S = BLACK

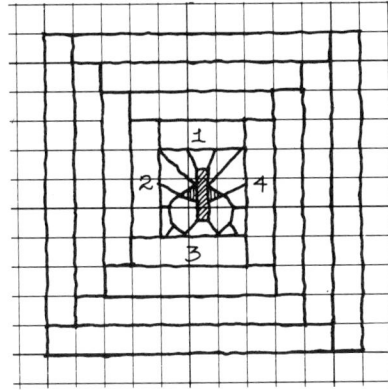

Tea Cozy with Butterflies —Handsewn

This tea cozy (see the photograph on page 48) should fit a six- to eight-cup teapot. It is sewn entirely in patchwork with the same design front and back.

Materials: Pattern paper. Various cotton remnants. Bias strips, about 49¼ inches (125 cm). Black shoelaces. Felt for the inside of the cozy.

Sewing and Finishing Instructions:

a. Following the pattern sketch, draw the pattern on pattern paper: on four-to-the-inch paper, you will have a design 9 inches × 12 inches (23 cm × 30.5 cm). If this seems too small, enlarge □ = 2 on ten-to-the-inch paper for a cozy about 11 inches × 14 inches (28 cm × 35.5 cm).

b. Plan the layout of the materials. Then mark the individual parts. I have used nine different fabrics, three of which are predominantly black.

c. Cut out the front, then the back, and sew, following Technique 1. Use your whole piece as a pattern for the inner felt cozy, front and back.

d. Press the pieces, remove the pattern papers, and baste on a length of bias stripping on one side to serve as a "peekaboo" border (see step 4b, page 78). Insert "antennae" of shoelaces. Machine-stitch the bias strip, first where basted and then to the other side.

e. Sew the felt liner together. Insert in cozy; baste lower edge if necessary. Finish edges with a bias-strip border. Press.

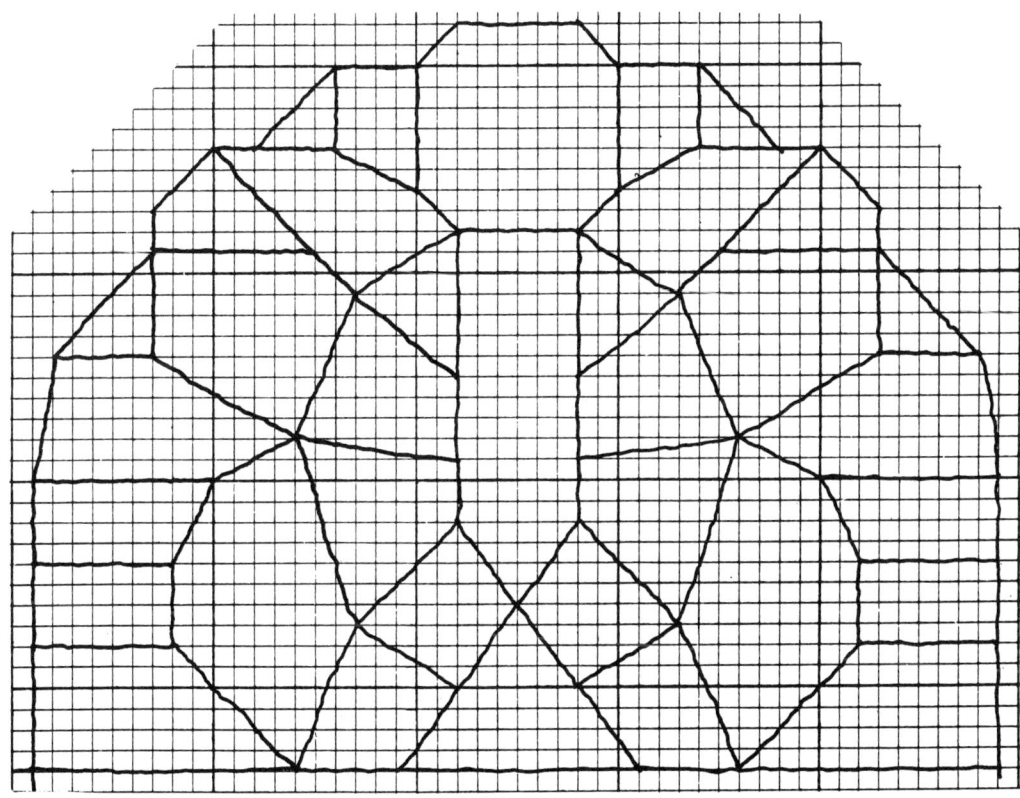

Butterfly in Ring—Handsewn

Materials: Pattern paper. Various cotton fabric remnants or scraps. Silver thread. Black beads (small). Hoop or wrought-iron ring, diameter about 20–22 inches (51 cm–56 cm).

Sewing and Finishing Instructions:

a. Draw the butterfly on pattern paper, following the pattern sketch: ☐ = 3.

b. Choose material. Here, black is marked S, SA; four light blue are marked B, BA, BB, BC; three strong blue, BS, BT, and BK; and two green are marked G, Gr. Mark the parts according to your own layout. See the color photograph on page 40.

c. Cut the papers, and sew the butterfly, following Technique 1. Press, and remove the papers.

d. Mount with a zigzag stitch (see page 79).

e. Stretch the butterfly out in the iron ring or hoop: Start by fastening the antennae. String the black beads; let the thread pass around the ring and back through the beads, through the material (see sketch), above the ring, repeating all the way around ending at the antennae. Before the final stitching, adjust and tighten the silver thread until the butterfly hovers in the middle of the ring. Fasten off.

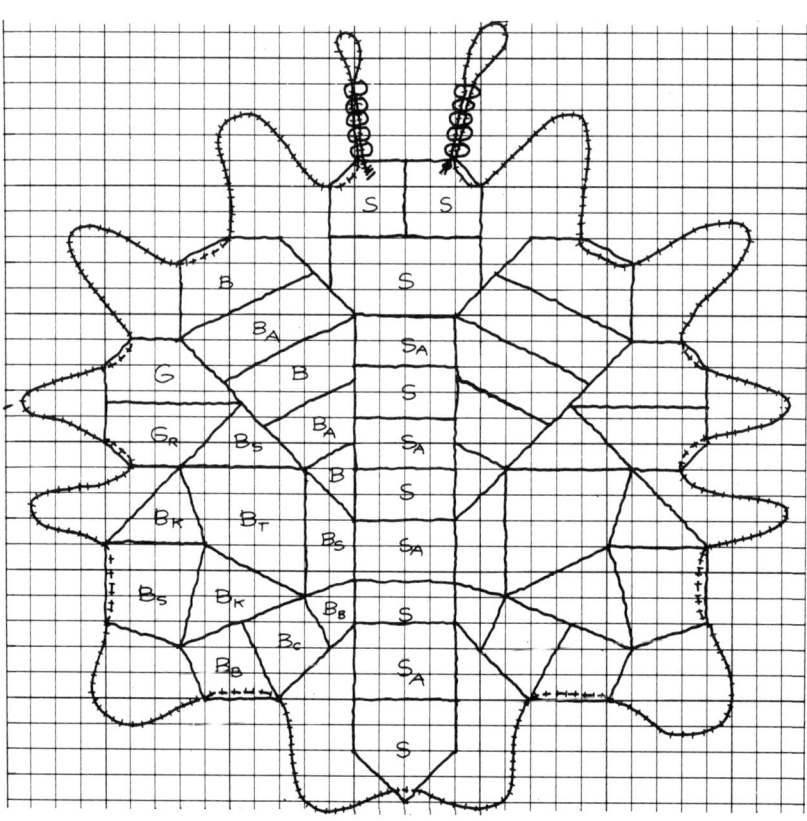

BLACK :   S , SA
LIGHT BLUE :   B, BA, BB, BC
STRONG BLUE : BS, BT, BK
GREEN :   G, GR

Table Mat with Butterflies
—Handsewn

This small table mat is the product of playing with a hexagon. It may be used as a runner on top of a light summer tablecloth. It is sewn of cotton fabric. Drawing the pattern is complicated, which makes this an advanced project.

Sewing and Finishing Instructions:
a. Draw a hexagon with a radius of 1¾ inches (4.5 cm) on tablet-back or shirt cardboard (Technique 2).
b. Use the pattern to draw a center hexagon and then six hexagons around it in a flower pattern. Following the sketch at right, draw a butterfly in each of the outer hexagons. Look at the diagram on page 72, and replace the diamonds formed where your butterfly hexagons meet with a smaller hexagon. Dash lines on the diagram show the original hexagon joinings. Next, construct a flower in the center hexagon by means of six small hexagons within the center hexagon, which then have their inner angles replaced by straight lines, creating another, turned hexagon for the flower center. See sketches below.

c. Choose material. I chose to make six identical butterflies. Mark the individual parts, cut out, and sew, following Technique 1. Mark inner and outer edges.
d. Press, remove paper, and mount, using an easy zigzag edge (see page 79). If necessary, top-stitch the butterfly by machine.

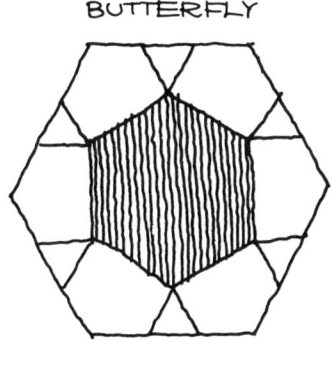

BUTTERFLY

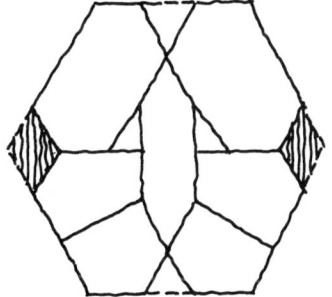

SOLID FLOWER CENTER

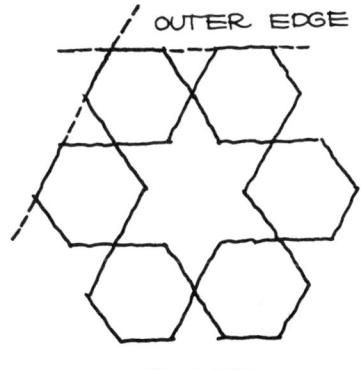

OUTER EDGE

FLOWER

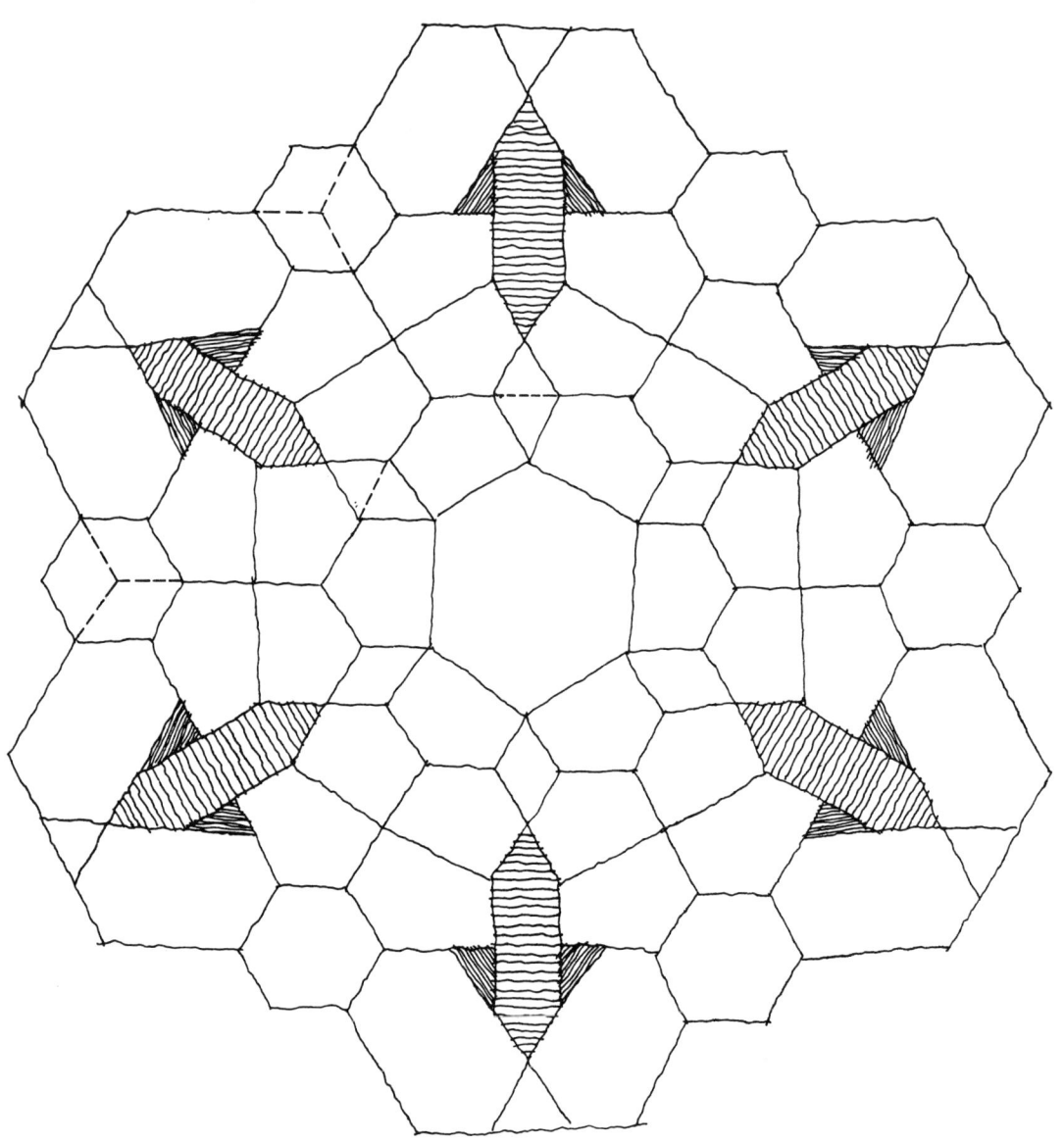

72

Easter Runner—Handsewn

Materials: Pattern paper. Cotton fabric: light yellow/green colors. Backing fabric, 15¾ inches × 62¼ inches (40 cm × 158 cm). Bias strips, about 4¼ yards (4 m).

Final Measurements: About 15 inches × 61½ inches (38 cm × 56.25 cm).

Sewing and Finishing Instructions:

a. Consult the pattern drawing on page 74. Draw the individual parts on pattern paper □ = 6, and cut as many of each piece as you need (see the list on page 74, right). If any of the pieces are to be laterally reversed (turned over, pivoting on one side), this is indicated by a plus sign (+) between the numerals.

b. Compose the oval eggs from the parts, and mount the background pieces in place on your worktable. Choose materials. Vary the colors you choose for the egg "white." See the color photograph on page 32.

c. Cut and sew, following Technique 1. Stay-stitch around the outside edges.

d. Baste a folded bias strip along the edge so that 3/16 inch or so (5 mm) is visible. Machine-stitch.

e. Cut lining with ⅝-inch (1-cm) seam allowance. Fold under, baste, and finally sew the lining to the stitched bias strip with small, blind hemstitches. Keep checking to be sure the lining is not visible from the front. Press.

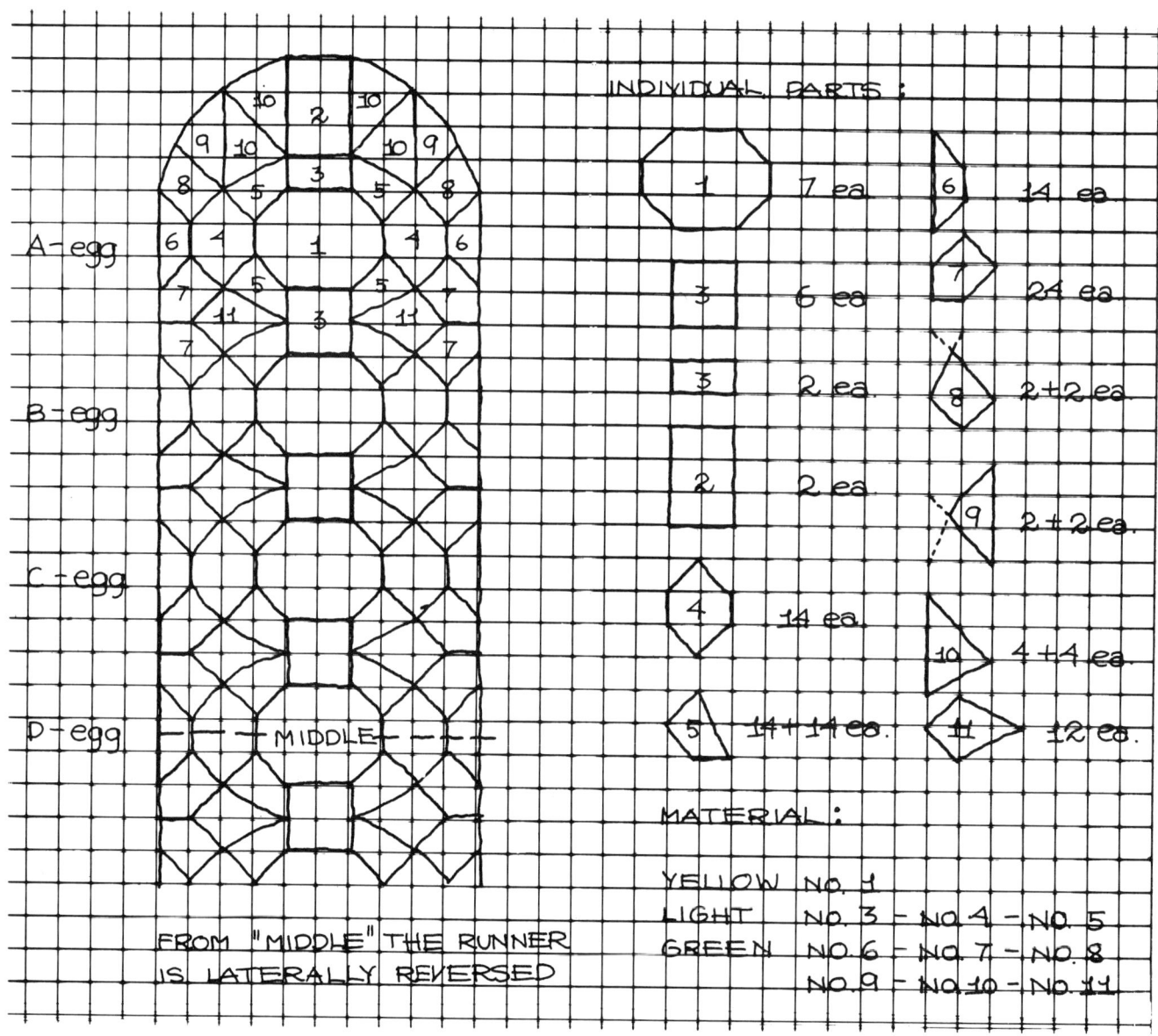

INDIVIDUAL PARTS:

A-egg

B-egg

C-egg

D-egg — — — — MIDDLE — — — —

FROM "MIDDLE" THE RUNNER
IS LATERALLY REVERSED

Part	Quantity	Part	Quantity
1	7 ea	6	14 ea
3	6 ea	7	24 ea
3	2 ea.	8	2+2 ea
2	2 ea.	9	2+2 ea.
4	14 ea	10	4+4 ea.
5	14+14 ea.	11	12 ea.

MATERIAL:

YELLOW NO. 1
LIGHT   NO. 3 - NO. 4 - NO. 5
GREEN   NO. 6 - NO. 7 - NO. 8
        NO. 9 - NO. 10 - NO. 11

74

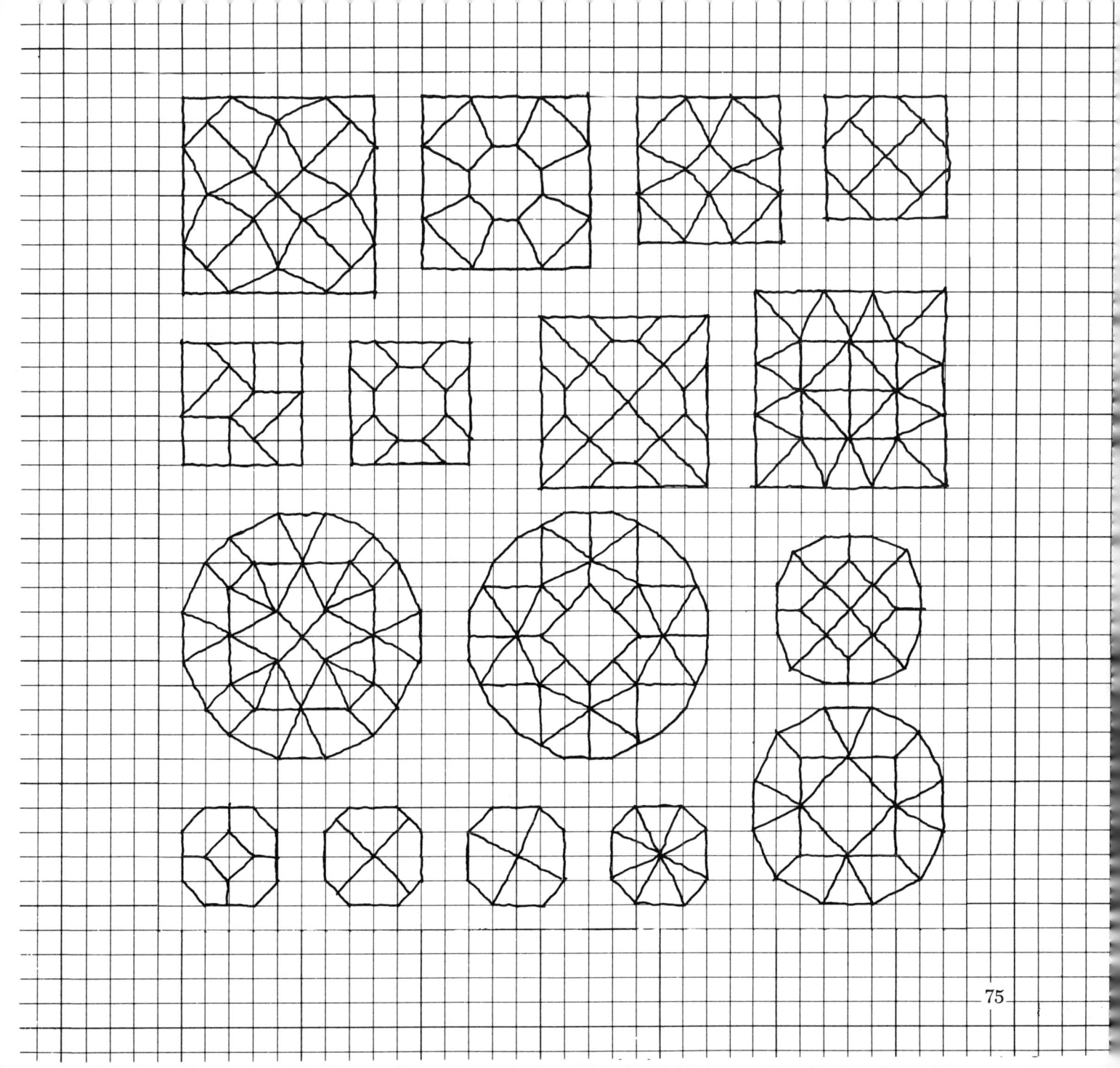

75

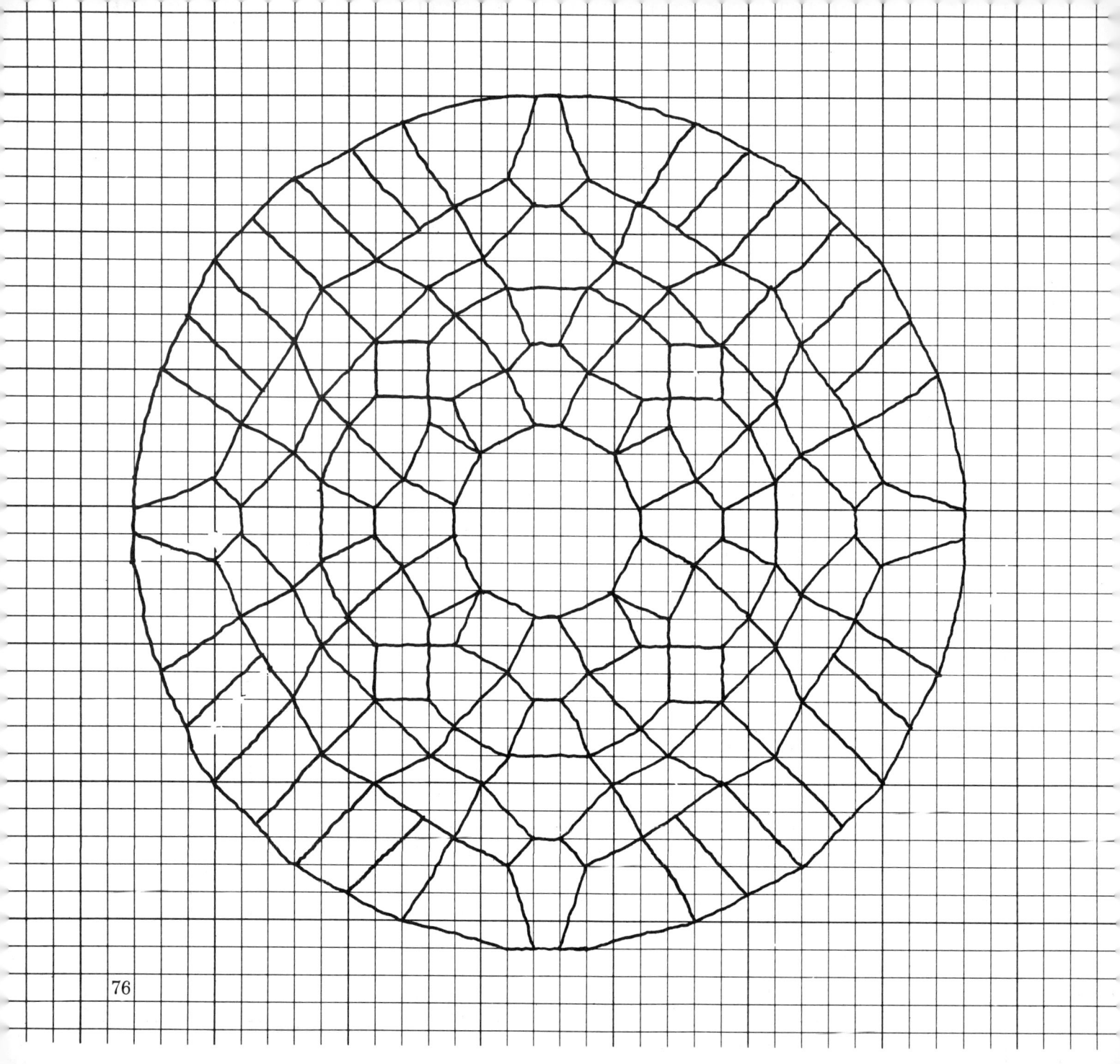

76

GENERAL INSTRUCTIONS FOR MOUNTING AND FINISHING

Mounting Wall Hangings with Borders and Mitered Corners

Border and back are cut in one piece of fabric.

Measurements: Finished size wanted plus twice the width of the finished border plus twice the seam allowance (normally ⅝ inch [1.5 cm]).

1. Fold the seam allowance under and then fold half of the border to the front along two sides. Press.
2. Make the corner as follows:
   a. Fold excess corner material (* to *), so that a diagonal fold line indicates where the seam is to be sewn. Be very careful.

b. Spread out the corner material and pin along the fold line through both thicknesses. Allow ⅜ inch (1 cm) for the seam. Trim away the excess.
c. With seam allowances to the front, press the seams apart, then turn them under and press from the front.
d. Sew the seam from the front with tiny stitches.
Repeat for the other three corners.

3. If desired, insert batting between backing and front. Finally, baste the tapestry or wall-hanging being framed (see page 81) along the sides, and stitch the border over the wall-hanging from the front. Then quilt if desired.

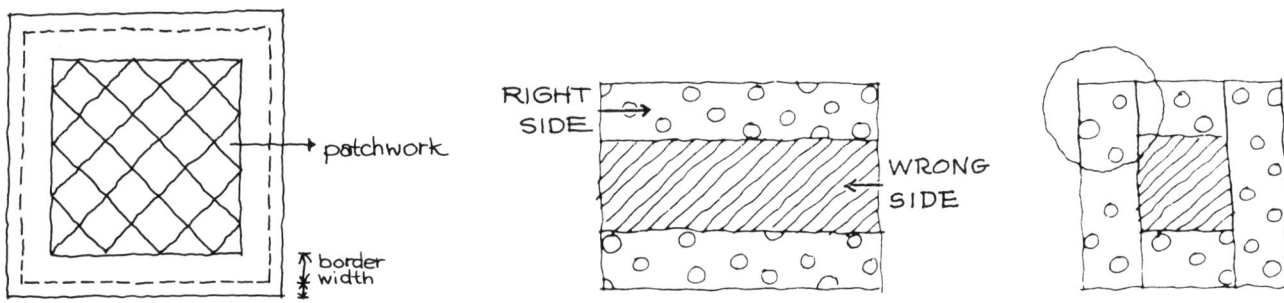

patchwork

border width

RIGHT SIDE

WRONG SIDE

TUCK IN THE CORNERS AS FOLLOWS

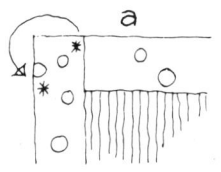

a

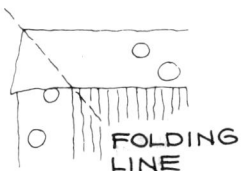

FOLDING LINE

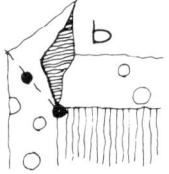

b

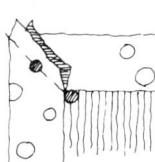

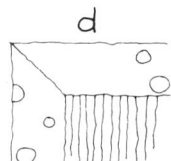

d

Mounting Pillows or Cushions

These finishing instructions are for a handsewn patchwork pillow about 16 inches square (41 × 41 cm), with a "peekaboo" border if desired, and a zipper. They can be adapted for other sizes by varying the dimensions slightly.

1. Cut the back to the size of the front plus seam allowances of ⅜ inch (1 cm) on three sides and 1³⁄₁₆ inch (3 cm) on the fourth (zipper) side.
2. Divide across the back by cutting at one-third the height of the pillow, as shown below. Stitch the two pieces together, right sides together, about 3½ inches (10 cm) in from each side, leaving an unsewn slit about 9 inches (23 cm) long. From the wrong side, press the seam open. Baste the zipper over the unsewn portion of the seam, and stitch in by hand or machine.
3. Fold and press back seam allowances so that the back is the same size as the front piece. Baste if necessary.
4. a. Remove any pattern papers from the front. Join front and back pieces with pins, and then stitch just inside the edge along the four sides of the cushion or pillow. Press.

   OR

   b. If desired, baste a "peekaboo" border of bias strips all around the front. Start in the middle of the lowest side; be careful with the corners, and tuck under the raw edges of the border strip before they are joined. Sew the border onto the front by hand with small blind-stitches. Then sew onto the back.

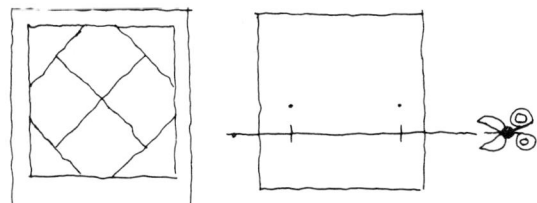

These finishing instructions can be used for hand- or machine-sewn patchwork pillows about 16 inches square (41 × 41 cm) if a Log Cabin border is desired.

1. Remove any pattern papers from the front. Press the seam allowances under. Fold a piece of ground fabric 16½ inches square (42 × 42 cm) diagonally from opposite corners to mark where the corners of the patchwork piece should fall. Baste the piece onto the ground fabric.
2. Tear strips the length of a side of the ground-fabric square plus ½ inch (1.5 cm), and to the desired width plus ½ inch (1.5 cm). Press in the direction of the lengthwise threads.
3. Sew the strips around the patchwork piece, right sides together, as follows: begin with the bottom edge, as for Log Cabin (Technique 9). Fold the right edge of the first strip back toward the center and pin for the moment. Sew on remaining strips. Then unpin the free edge of the first strip and turn it over the fourth strip. Stitch the small final seam. Topstitch inside the edge on all four sides and trim excess material on the back if necessary. Press.

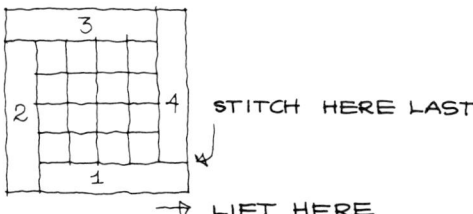

4. Cut the back piece 16½ inches square (42 × 42 cm). Place it right sides together against the front piece and stitch ¼ inch (6 mm) from the raw edges, beginning about 4 inches (12 cm) before a corner, and continuing around three sides and about 4 inches (12 cm) into the side you began with, leaving an opening as shown in the sketch. Trim the corners as shown.

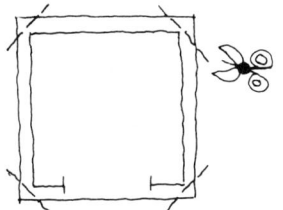

Finally, turn right-side-out and press.

5. Insert the cushion filler and sew the bottom slit together with blind overcast stitches.

Mounting a Tea Cozy

Materials: Cotton fabric for lining. Felt for the inner cozy.

1. Cut two inner cozies to the size of the finished cozy (no seam allowances). Zigzag the pieces together. Stitch again ¼ inch (6 mm) from the zigzagged edges. Insert it into the tea cozy and, if necessary, adjust the lower edge: it must not be seen. Remove.
2. Cut two lining pieces to the size of the inner cozy but adding 1½ inches (4 cm) to the bottom edges. Right sides together, stitch ¼ inch (6 mm) from the edge after zigzagging as before. Insert the lining into the inner cozy. Tuck the edges of the lining around the bottom edge of the inner cozy and
3. Insert the inner cozy with lining in the outer tea cozy.

Overlapped Cushion Closing

Sew the cushion back as follows:
1. Cut two back pieces the same width as the front (including seam allowances), but with the height equal to one-half that of the front plus about 3 inches (7.6 cm). Therefore, if the cushion front is 16 inches square (41 × 41 cm), cut two pieces 16 inches × 11 inches (41 × 28 cm).

2. Stitch a narrow double seam on the pieces (so that no raw edges are left) on the sides toward the middle.
3. Place the two sides in position over the front piece, right sides together. The two pieces will overlap by at least 2 inches (5 cm). Pin. Stitch the cushion on all four sides about ⅜ inch (1 cm) from the raw edges.
4. Trim corners, turn right-side-out, and press.

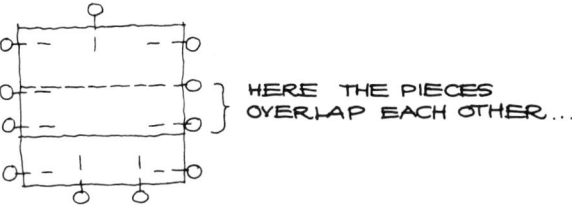

HERE THE PIECES OVERLAP EACH OTHER...

Easy Zigzag Mounting

1. Remove tacking threads and pattern papers from the front. Baste the edges of the patchwork piece. If necessary, press.
2. Cut back fabric the same size as the patchwork front plus ⅜ inch (1 cm) for seam allowance.
3. Tuck in the seam and baste on the back. It must be invisible from the right side.
4. Zigzag by machine all the way around. The needle must fall just outside the material on the outer edge.

MATERIAL

MORE ABOUT PATCHWORK TECHNIQUES AND SUPPLIES

Choosing Colors and Fabrics

Always choose fabric and colors based on one central idea. Realize what you find most important in your own pattern: the center section? the corners? perhaps a circle formed by the pattern? Give this part a conspicuous color (strong/very dark/very light). Lay out a small pattern on your worktable or cork board in your first choice of materials. If necessary, replace some fabrics to get better or more interesting combinations. Don't forget that colors are very much affected by surrounding colors. Colors unsuitable for the position you've placed them in will often show up when you squint a bit at your layout: they "leap to the eye" from the other colors.

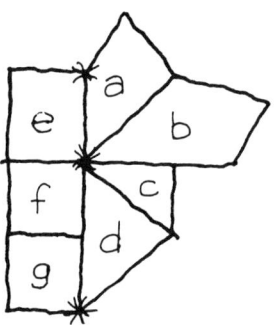

How Much Material?

I have not specified the amount of fabric needed for the patchwork designs in this book, because it is very often small scraps that you use for patchwork. For large projects, such as bedcovers, you can calculate the amount roughly by placing cardboard pattern templates as economically as you can (but with regard to one-way designs, grain, and so forth) on the full width of the fabric excluding selvage edges, and multiplying according to how many sets of pieces you need. This procedure requires time and patience, but who isn't annoyed or worse at running out of material before a project is finished? Overestimate rather than underestimate: you'll doubtless find a use for any leftover material.

Yardage has been given for major pieces required for a pattern, such as ground fabric or mounting.

Stitching Sequence

It is often wise to sew the individual patchwork pieces into the units or modules you divided them down from when you devised your pattern. Later, join the modules, being sure to line up seams, keep crisp angles, and so forth. Sew straight lines instead of in and out of angles whenever possible.

Example: Sew parts a and b together to form a right angle. Sew c and d together to form a right angle. Sew the a–b unit to the c–d unit where the right angles meet (the middle * in the sketch). Sew e to f and f to g to make a strip. Then sew the straight seam from the top joining of e and a (*) down to the lower joining of g and d (*).

These rules hold for machine *and* hand piecing.

About Quilting

To quilt means to sew together a fabric "sandwich" of front or top, padding, and backing.

Quilting is an ancient skill with many traditions. Books on the history and technique of quilting are available at your library.

Quilting gives needlework a textured, shadowed surface. Quilting can change the character of needlework completely, depending on how it is done.

For padding, you can use terry cloth, polyester batting (be sure it is bonded), cotton batting, or even a blanket.

For quilting, you may use doubled sewing thread, embroidery cotton, cotton thread, metallic thread, thread reinforced with beeswax, or whatever pleases you, depending on how you want to use the finished project. Heavier use requires sturdier thread. "Quilting thread" is now widely available.

Prepare Your Work for Quilting:

Cut a backing piece to the finished size desired plus a seam allowance of about ¾ inch (2 cm)—the larger the piece, the larger the seam allowance needed. Place the backing wrong-side-up on your worktable, then line up your padding over it, and complete the fabric "sandwich" with your patchwork piece, right-side-up. The padding should be the same size as your backing piece.

Baste from the middle of the piece toward the corners through all three layers, keeping the piece flat on the table as you work. Then baste from the middle toward the sides. Be sure to tighten the basting threads as you go to hold the three layers together firmly (but not so tightly as to distort the piece). If your piece is large, run more basting lines outward from the center in between those you've already sewn. Large diagonal stitches work well.

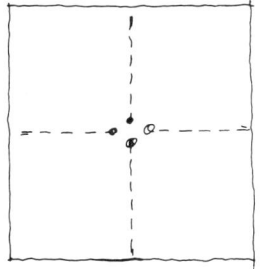

BASTE CENTERLINES

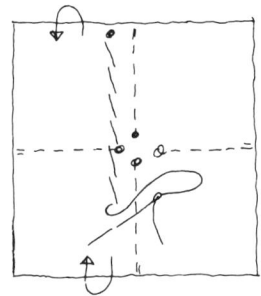

FELLING STITCHES
SEW UP AND DOWN

Draw quilting lines (see pattern or photograph) with a white marking pencil or chalk (you can use soft ordinary lead pencil on light fabrics as long as you plan to wash the piece after it is quilted).

Machine-Quilt:

Use long stitches and make use of the sewing machine accessories (seam width guide, presser foot, and quilting foot if you have one). Consult the sewing machine manual.

Trim the sides of the top, batting, and backing, remove the basting, and mount a zigzag border.

OR

Zigzag backing, batting, and patchwork top together. Trim clean, remove basting, and finish according to the pattern instructions.

81

Bias Strips as Finishing

Bias strips (bias bindings and borders) are used to finish the edges of work, especially quilted pieces. Choose the width of the bias strip according to the thickness of the border to be sewn and the effect you want:

The strip is to be visible on front and back. Fold the strip in the middle and sew it to front and back with one line of stitching. Miter corners (below).

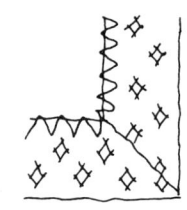

ZIG-ZAG
MACHINE MADE

The whole strip is to be visible from the front side. Position the strip on the piece right-side-down on the wrong side of the work. Stitch near the edge leaving a small seam allowance, then turn the strip to the front and machine-stitch, mitering corners (below).

Corners. These corners are sewn in a single operation; if necessary, baste first. Begin by folding the strip in the middle. Tuck under the triangle of excess material on front and back where you turn the corner, making a diagonal line from the corner.

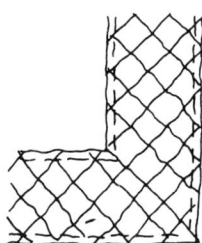

NORMAL
MACHINE-
STITCHING

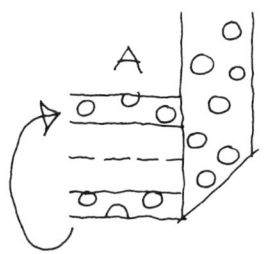

A

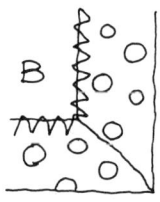

B

You can buy bias strips in many solid colors and shades, or with a small print; or you can make your own as described in Technique 10, using "patchwork" combinations of strips of several fabrics or strips of only one fabric as you please.

Some variations are shown in the following.

BY HAND:
NORMAL
STITCHING

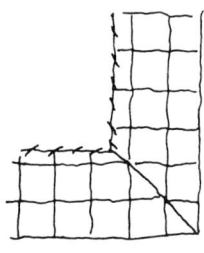

SEW WITH
BLIND HEMSTITCHING

ROUND THE CORNERS
OF THE MATERIAL
BEFORE SEWING ON-
STRETCH THE OUTER EDGE
A LITTLE ON THE BIAS STRIP

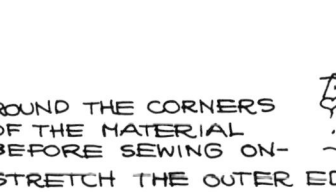
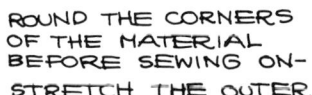

Padded Buttons

Find a large trouser button. Cut material twice the width of the button plus ⅜ inch (1 cm). Tuck in a small, narrow seam all the way around (see sketch). Place batting or a bit of cotton or wool on the front of the button to puff up the material when you place it, right side up, on top of the button, so that it curves well. Run a strong thread through the small seam around the circumference, and tighten. Sew a few stitches to secure the material, and sew on the button with the thread.

If the padded button is sewn on the front of a cushion, you will want to sew a small button opposite it on the back.

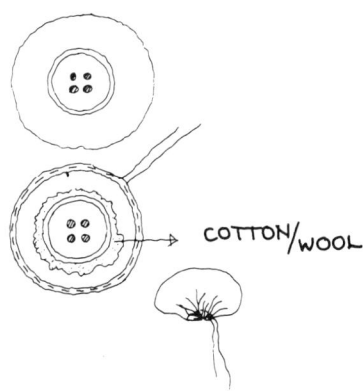

COTTON/WOOL

Dividing the Pieces in Your Pattern Drawing

1. Use the squares on the pattern paper to draw from corner to corner over one, two, or three squares. This will make the design easier to enlarge later on.
2. Never divide a right angle (90°) into more than three angles. The more acute (sharp) the angles, the more difficult it is to make them precise.
3. Draw the individual parts as equal in size as possible (especially if you are a beginner).
4. Obtuse angles (those larger than 90°) cannot be sewn easily or smoothly. If they turn up in your design, divide them down further as shown below.

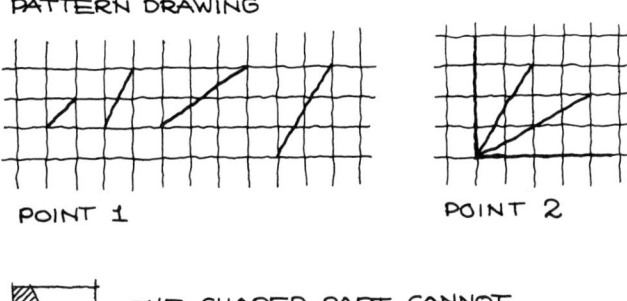

PATTERN DRAWING

POINT 1   POINT 2

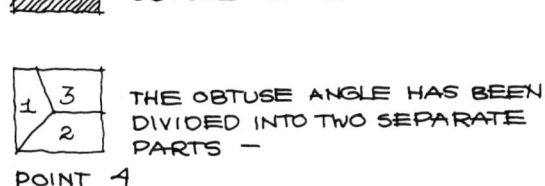

THE SHADED PART CANNOT BE SEWN BECAUSE OF THE OBTUSE ANGLE –

THE OBTUSE ANGLE HAS BEEN DIVIDED INTO TWO SEPARATE PARTS –

POINT 4

A NOTE ABOUT ENLARGEMENT: If you are ruling out patter paper yourself for a design that is to be enlarged, you can save work by drawing the squares to the enlarged size and then simply following your pattern sketch. For example, if your enlargement is □ = 4, draw a square 4 squares × 4 on your original grid and then rule out your own paper to the size of the new square. In several patterns, □ = 4 gives a new square of 1 inch—an easy size to rule out yourself.

Basting

Basting Acute Angles

Follow the steps in the drawings at right, leaving seam allowances loose as shown.

Basting of Outer Edges for Machine Sewing

If you are sewing patchwork that will later be mounted by machine, save time by leaving the seam allowances on what will be the outer edge of the piece free instead of basting around the pattern paper. You will already have indicated for yourself which edges fall on the outside with a wavy line Technique 5). Baste only the single thickness of fabric near the edge to the paper pattern.

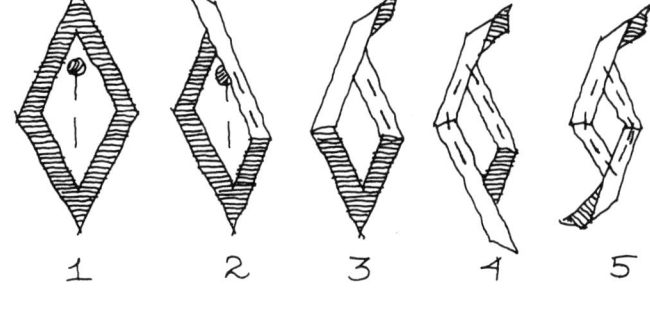

OUTER EDGE

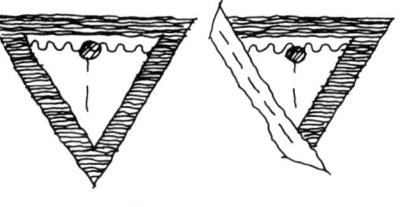

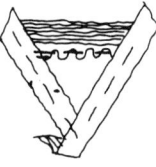

BASTE THROUGH WITHOUT TUCKING IN THE SEAM IN ORDER TO SECURE THE MATERIAL

Preparing Pieces for Appliqué— "Clean Sewing"

When you sew patchwork that will later be appliquéd on backing material, or if you want to sew the outer edges clean (that is, without raw edges or seam allowances left free), simply indicate the outer edges with a straight line as you have indicated the other edges of the piece, and end your basting on the outside edge. Then the outer seam allowance will automatically turn inward, leaving the edge finished. See the sketch.

TOWARDS EDGE

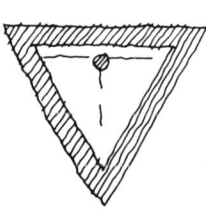

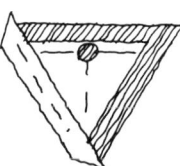

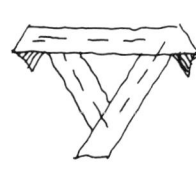

Quick Ways of Experimenting

When you need to get a rough idea of how your pattern is developing, you will find a few fast methods of appraising your progress useful: you'll certainly want a quicker method than sewing it up. However, large pieces built up by modules are partial exceptions: for these, it is probably best to test a module by basting fabric over pattern pieces, pressing, and mounting on your cork layout board with pins—without completing the sewing.

Checking Pattern Distribution:

Using the same fabrics in different parts of the design, look at the effect of different prints used together.

Use a squiggle or some kind of sketchy drawing or doodle to indicate the kind and size of print you are considering. Think of these indicators as though they were the symbols denoting color areas in cross-stitch embroidery. Make notes about particular fabrics. Let yourself be inspired by the material. Here are ten examples:

Checking Color Distribution:

Show light/dark color effects with a color sketch. Color your pattern with ordinary colored pencils—color them on top of each other, mix them; press hard or press softly. This method is especially suitable for modules that are to be reversed, and which will then produce new overall patterns. It is not always easy to foresee the effect of color distribution.

Small Designs

For small designs, it is useful to glue material right onto your traced pattern. But don't mount tiny patches of each fabric in the middle of pattern pieces: this doesn't give any impression of how the colors and prints work together when they actually touch. Glue material on the entire surface, so that the ratio of colors is correct—the effect of each color depends both on its surroundings and on the size of the piece used. It takes little time to glue material onto the sketch and to decide which materials will give the effect you want.

Buying and Using Fabric

The fabric you will use will very often be cotton fabric that can be torn easily along the warp or the weft—that is, along grain lines. If you choose colors that are not particularly fashionable that season, you can probably find material offered at a low price. If I am not planning to start on a major work or use the material for mounting a large piece, I rarely buy more than ½ yard (about 45 cm), which will go a very long way. In most shops, clerks will willingly tear the fabric off the bolt for you.

Prewashing

Material used for patchwork that is later to be washed must always be washed before sewing.

This washing removes starch, and material may shrink as a result. Because fabrics are woven with different thread counts (the denseness, or number of fibers woven per inch) and from different materials, they will also shrink differently—by five to ten percent; and this makes preshrinking necessary. It is also possible that some colors in the fabric may run—especially dark colors. Although the dye may run again in subsequent washings, the problem will not be so acute, and the dye will be unlikely to stain other fabrics or color areas.

Layout Board

Use soft Celotex (bulletin board material) or decorator cork tiles covered with sheeting or other neutral cotton fabric. Tighten the linen, and fasten with pins, staples, or thumbtacks on the back.

I myself use many small boards, about 15 inches × 18 inches (38 cm × 45 cm); they are handy and can be carried around easily. For tapestries, I use large boards, 32 inches × 39 inches (about 80 cm × 100 cm).

Pattern Paper

For my paper pattern pieces, I use paper of about construction paper weight that has been ruled out in 8-mm squares (a little more than three-squares-to-the-inch), which is available in Denmark in standard sheets. However, the instructions in this book have been converted to four-squares-to-the-inch paper, since this is the size readily available to Americans. For larger works, several or many sheets must be taped together before drawing the pattern, and some of the instructions for the projects in this book reflect this. All less-than-full squares are cut away and the squares are aligned sheet-to-sheet and taped from the back. The tape is easily pierced when basting. See the list of suppliers (page 89) for a source for four-to-the-inch paper of the proper weight.

GLOSSARY

Acute angle—An angle of less than 90°.

Batting—Here, synthetic batting, a pad of woolly or cottony fiber used between the layers of quilts. Cotton batting is also available, but requires more quilting than synthetic batting to hold it in place. Whichever you choose, be sure the batting is "bonded."

Bias—The diagonal direction across the grain of fabric. If lengthwise and widthwise threads meet at a right angle, the bias corresponds to the imaginary line that could be drawn opposite that right angle to make a triangle.

Bisect—To divide into two exactly equal parts.

Color value—The density of the color of material as it is affected by its surroundings.

Diameter—The line that can be drawn from one side of a circle to the opposite side to divide it exactly in half: it equals two times the radius.

Double seam—A finished seam made by turning the raw edges of the seam allowance under and then under once again, both seam allowances pressed to the same side, so that no raw edges will be visible once a line of stitching is done close to the folded-under edge of the seam allowance. This is the kind of seam used inside jeans, for example.

Hobby knife—A single-edged blade mounted in a handle; it is used for many crafts and is widely available (X-ACTO® -knife, for example).

Interlining—The layer between the patchwork top and the backing: batting, terry cloth, and so on.

Miter—To make an angled corner where a vertical and a horizontal strip meet: the seam between them makes a diagonal line from the outer to the inner corner.

Module—A unit made up of one or many parts that is repeated to make up an overall pattern.

Obtuse angle—An angle larger than 90°.

Primary module—The most important (and usually the largest) unit to be repeated for your design: the one you want to emphasize.

Radius—The line from the center of a circle to its circumference: one-half the diameter.

Right angle—An angle of exactly 90°.

Secondary module—The smaller unit repeated for your design, usually smaller than the primary module and often formed by the space between primary modules.

Stitch—To sew an ordinary straight seam by machine.

SUPPLIERS

Batting and Pillow Forms

Fairfield Processing Corporation
P.O. Box 1130
Danbury, CT 06810

Polyfil®, Extra-Loft®, Ultra-Loft®, and Cotton Classic
   Batting
   Soft 'n Crafty®, and Pop-in-Pillow® pillow forms

Stearns & Foster Company
P.O. Box 15380
Cincinnati, OH 45215

Mountain Mist® Bleached Cotton Batting, Mountain
   Mist® Cotton Gold, Mountain Mist® Polyester Bat-
   ting, and Mountain Mist® Fatt Batt.
   Mountain Mist® Pillowloft pillow forms

Fabrics

Concord Fabrics, Inc.
1411 Broadway
New York, NY 10018

Peter Pan Fabrics
Henry Glass & Company
1071 Sixth Avenue
New York, NY 10018

Graph Paper

BLD Enterprises
Betty L. Donahue
2624 West 155th Street
Gardena, CA 90249
(213) 324-2446

BLD can supply grid sheets heavy enough to hold the shape of your pattern pieces yet light enough to sew through easily. Ask for 4-to-the-inch grid sheets printed on index stock. Available by the sheet in 11″ × 17″, 9″ × 12″, and 8½″ × 11″ sheets. BLD has an impressive line of graph paper and grids suitable for all kinds of crafts projects.